D0362458

Care
and
Moral
Motivation

BJ 1475 S56   [NLRC]
C. 1
CARE AND MORAL MOTIVATION

M7/1407535

DATE DUE

**Three (3) week loans are subject
to recall after one week**

NOV 3 1994		
DEC 16 1994		
FEB 22 1995		
MAY 9 1995		
JUL 19 1995		
AUG 8 1995		

AUG - 6 1992

Care
and
Moral
Motivation

Debra Shogan

Monograph Series / 20

OISE Press

The Ontario Institute for Studies in Education

BJ
1475
S56

The Ontario Institute for Studies in Education has three prime functions: to conduct programs of graduate study in education, to undertake research in education, and to assist in the implementation of the findings of educational studies. The Institute is a college chartered by an Act of the Ontario Legislature in 1965. It is affiliated with the University of Toronto for graduate studies purposes.

The publications program of the Institute has been established to make available information and materials arising from studies in education, to foster the spirit of critical inquiry, and to provide a forum for the exchange of ideas about education. The opinions expressed should be viewed as those of the contributors.

© The Ontario Institute for Studies in Education 1988
252 Bloor Street West
Toronto, Ontario
M5S 1V6

All rights reserved. No part of this publication may be reproduced in any form without permission from the publisher, except for brief passages quoted for review purposes.

Canadian Cataloguing in Publication Data
Shogan, Debra A., 1951-
  Care and moral motivation

(Monograph series ; 20)
Bibliography: p.
ISBN 0-7744-0325-X

1. Ethics. 2. Moral education. 3. Caring.
I. Title. II. Series: Monograph series (Ontario
Institute for Studies in Education) ; 20.

BJ1475.S56 1988   170   C88-095051-X

All possible care has been taken to trace ownership and obtain permission for copyright material used. If any errors or omissions have occurred, they will be corrected in subsequent editions, provided they are brought to the publisher's attention.

ISBN 0-7744-0325-X   Printed in Canada
1 2 3 4 5 WC 29 19 09 98 88

Contents

∞ Preface ∞

The title of this book — *Care and Moral Motivation* — reflects my dual interest in ethics and moral education. This is a work in ethics insofar as it addresses what it is to be a moral agent and what is involved in moral motivation. It is a work in moral education insofar as it is concerned with how people can be motivated to be *morally* motivated. My interest in moral motivation took a different direction with the release of Carol Gilligan's important book on care. Her work fuelled my discontent with traditional accounts of morality as well as my interest in accounting for women's experiences of moral agency. What was exciting for me was that I was able to pursue my interest in moral motivation while attempting to come to a more clear understanding of what care is. My account of care turns out to be different in important respects from Gilligan's, but I am indebted to insights from her work which suggested to me ways in which care, as a moral phenomenon, could help account for the centrality of moral motivation to a moral life. I took on this project as my Ph.D. dissertation in the Philosophy of Education at the University of Alberta. For helpful direction during that process, I am grateful to the members of my committee, particularly my advisor, Ivan DeFaveri.

The original manuscript has undergone some important changes as a result of discussions I was fortunate to have while on study leave at The Ontario Institute for Studies in Education in the fall of 1986. I would like to thank Dwight Boyd and Ruth Pierson and others in the Centre for Women's Studies in Education for commenting on presentations based on this work which I made while I was at OISE. I particularly benefitted from conversations I had during this time with my very good friend and colleague, Maureen Ford.

I have profited from comments others have shared with me as a result of presentations and articles submitted for publication over the past two years. I would like to thank William Hare for his comments on a paper on moral emotions which I presented at the Learned Societies' Meetings in Hamilton in June 1987, and Barbara Houston and Susan Sherwin for suggestions made to a paper on gender and moral agency which I submitted to *Atlantis: A Journal of Women's Studies*. As well I am grateful for the direction provided by the anonymous reviewers from the Canadian Federation for the Humanities.

I want to acknowledge the support of my community of friends in Edmonton, particularly Wendy Bedingfield, Laura Cabott, Helen Greaves, and Jane Watkinson. Special thanks to my colleague and caring friend, Cathy Bray, whose day-to-day presence has been instrumental to the completion of this project.

Parts of this work have appeared recently in other publications. I would like to thank the editors of *New Education* for permitting me to use portions of "Moral Education in Schools: Theory Into Practice" (Vol. 8, No. 2, 1986) in chapter 6, the editors of *The Canadian Journal of Feminist Ethics* for the use in chapter 5 of a review of Nel Noddings's book, *Caring: A Feminine Approach to Ethics and Moral Education* (Vol. I, No. 2, 1986), and the editor of *Atlantis: A Journal of Women's Studies* (Vol. 13, No. 2, 1988) for permission to use parts of my article published there called "Gender and Moral Agency."

Debra Shogan
University of Alberta

Acknowledgment

This book has been published with the help of a grant from the Canadian Federation for the Humanities, using funds provided by the Social Sciences and Humanities Research Council of Canada.

I

A book about care might be expected to emphasize the moral significance of human concern and its emotional expression, the importance of human relations, and the role certain kinds of character traits play in the life of a caring person. While establishing these features of care, it might be expected that a sharp contrast would be made with those characteristics of moral life which have been emphasized in some traditional philosophy — namely, reason, autonomy, principle, and duty. This approach might be expected because most of the writing about care since Carol Gilligan's[1] important book has looked at care in this way.[2]

What is different about this book is that, while attempting to show that care is central to morality by emphasizing character traits, emotion, and relationships, I do not do this by reinforcing traditional dichotomies in moral philosophy — for example, between care and justice, care and principles, character and duty, motivation and action, friends and strangers, emotionality and rationality, connection and autonomy, or women's morality and men's morality. Rather, I attempt to show that care is central to morality for the very reason that it is able to accommodate many aspects of morality often thought to be dichotomous. I will briefly touch here on how I approach these dichotomies in the chapters to come.

1. *Care and Justice.* By establishing care as a motivational term, I will show that care is neither appropriately contrasted with justice nor appropriately made synonymous with benevolence, both of which are common assumptions. I will show that someone can both care that others are treated well and care that they are treated fairly.

2. *Care and Principles.* I establish a link between care and principles by showing that a caring person must, from time to time, refer to principles in order to respond to others in a moral situation. A caring per-

1

son may need to remind himself or herself of principles which justify care in a particular situation. Although the primary focus of a caring person is on those in a moral situation, there are times when he or she is not directly motivated to respond to them and, instead, desires to fulfill a duty which is based on caring principles (welfare and fair treatment of sentient beings). There are principles which justify care, but a caring person is not a principled person in the traditional sense because a caring person very often does not directly refer to principles in order to respond.

Sorting the place of principles in a caring person's life is complex, particularly if principles and justice are thought to be synonymous and justice is then contrasted with care. Care is not the opposite of principle. And, as I said above, care is not appropriately contrasted to justice either. Moreover, justice is not always appropriately aligned with principles.

3. *Character and Duty.* I will establish character traits as fairly permanent caring desires. A caring person is one who fairly permanently desires others' welfare and fair treatment. It is practically impossible, however, for someone directly to desire the welfare and fair treatment of all sentient beings in every moral situation. I will show that, in situations in which a caring person does not directly desire another's welfare or fair treatment, he or she acknowledges a duty based on principles which justify care in order to complete a caring response.

4. *Motivation and Action.* I am concerned to describe the total response of a caring person to a moral situation. In order to do this, I necessarily discuss both the motivation of the person who responds as well as what is done. I contend, however, that the nature of what is done cannot be adequately described without including motivation. Rather than separate motivation from action, what someone does is better understood by combining the two in a reference to a person's response.

5. *Friends and Strangers.* Studies, notably by Nel Noddings,[3] have circumscribed care within a series of concentric circles so that the further others are removed from a caring person, the less likely it is that this person will care about them. But I argue that proximity is neither a guarantee that someone will care nor a necessary barrier to it. I also discuss the inappropriateness of a notion like supererogation to deal adequately with our relations to those who are less proximate or who are in extraordinary moral situations.

6. *Emotionality and Rationality.* Rather than opt either for a moral response as coldly rational or as only emotional, I show that a caring

response is rationally based and that it necessarily consists of caring emotions which are conceptually linked to moral motivating reasons.

7. *Connection and Autonomy.* Neither connection nor autonomy are always appropriate ways to contend with others in moral situations. It must be established, on independent grounds, what is morally appropriate about each. I will argue that autonomy is important in situations in which fair adjudication of conflict is necessary and that underlying a caring person's response to this type of situation is a connection to those in the situation. Connection may be problematic, however, when the nature of the connection makes it impossible to be fair in a situation which requires fair treatment or when someone cannot respond at all to others except as a dependent member of a relationship. Autonomy may be problematic when the autonomous person is distant or uncommunicative, for example.

8. *Women's Morality and Men's Morality.* While recognizing the necessity of emphasizing that moral agency is an example of gendered experience, I argue for an understanding of care which, if not presently experienced in the same way by women and men, *can* be experienced by both, given significant social changes.

I use both feminine and masculine referents when discussing individual caring people who make caring responses in particular moral situations. I do this for two reasons. The first reason relates to the widely accepted view that exclusive use of masculine referents begs certain important questions. One of the more important of these is whether masculine referents can adequately reflect different experiences women and men tend to have of the social world. Because the socially constructed experiences of women and men are often very different, masculine referents are only accurately used in those situations which reflect men's experiences. Masculine, and not neutral referents, should be used in those situations which reflect men's experiences since it is misleading to use neutral words, such as people or humans, when masculine experience is discussed. Not only must masculine referents not be exclusively used when, by doing so, women's experiences are excluded, masculine references must not exclusively be used when an experience is one that both women and men could have.[4] If confusion is to be avoided about whose experience is being described, feminine and masculine referents must both be used when the experiences of women and men are not significantly distinguished by their gendered existence in the world. It is arguable, however, that in a world in which men are more valued than women, all experiences will be gendered experiences. I essentially agree with this position.

3

Why, then, do I use both feminine and masculine referents to describe caring people and caring responses, particularly when recent literature indicates that caring tends to describe women's experiences of the moral life and not men's experiences?[5] While understanding ways in which women and men live their moral lives is essential to an improved understanding of morality, it is important to be clear that descriptions of what women and men do in moral situations is not tantamount to what they ought to do. This work is an attempt to describe what people — women and men — do *if* they are caring people.

Accounts of caring which are important in the literature — namely, that of Carol Gilligan and Nel Noddings — are considerably different from my own motivational account. A motivational account of caring can accommodate gendered experiences of moral agency while, at the same time, show that, if descriptions of what women and men do in moral situations are accurate, these gendered experiences are not always indicative of care.

One purpose of this book is to dissolve dichotomies by explicating care as a motivational term. The other purpose is to discuss how a person can be motivated to care — or, in other words, to address the question how moral motivation can itself be motivated.

It will be useful to introduce here an outline of what will follow in the remaining chapters. In chapter 2, I introduce an argument for understanding care as a motivational concept. In doing this, I contrast care as motivation to an ability to understand moral reasons. By showing that care is a particular kind of motivation and by establishing character traits as fairly permanent motivation, I argue that someone who fairly permanently desires others' welfare and fair treatment is a caring person.

In chapter 3, I elaborate features of character traits which are essential to a caring person. I do this by differentiating moral situations into two basic types — those in which welfare is at stake and in which no adjudication is required and those in which adjudication is required to ensure fair treatment of those in a conflict. By arguing for the importance of responding to these fundamental moral situations, I show that there are two character traits central to a caring person: the fairly permanent desire that others' welfare is enhanced (benevolence), and the fairly permanent desire that others are treated fairly (justice). A caring person, I argue, is one who is both benevolent and just. It is in chapter 3 that I argue justice to be as important to care as is benevolence. I show here, as well, that care-principle and character-duty dichotomies are unfounded. I argue that not only is the justification of care based on principles which refer to welfare and fair treatment of sentient beings but also there are occasions in which a caring person must actively refer to these principles at the time of a moral

4

response in order to complete a response. An elaboration of this point allows me to show that a caring person (that is, a person who has certain character traits) acts, from time to time, according to recognized duties.

The inappropriateness of the act-motivation dichotomy is made clear in chapter 4 where I discuss the nature of a caring response. As part of this discussion, I am also able to show that there are at least four types of caring responses which are differentiated according to whether adjudication and reference to principles are required. In outlining these four caring responses, I am able to make the case for three types of moral reasons — moral motivating reasons, moral adjudicating reasons, and moral justifying reasons — as well as indicate the necessary role of emotions in each type of caring response. I also discuss extraordinary caring responses and, in doing so, make some comments about responses to friends and strangers.

In chapter 5, I address the issue of gendered differences in moral agency. I argue that, in order for care to be a moral response, it must not be a response only of girls and women. At the same time, however, I argue against dismissing gender as unimportant to a better understanding of moral philosophy. By examining gender and care, I am able to say something about the relative significance of connection and autonomy to a caring person.

There are occasions in which someone may be motivated to respond to others in a moral situation but not do so because of factors which interfere with the completion of a response. I discuss these factors in chapters 6 and 7, and examine how education might have an effect on each. Chapter 7, however, is concerned predominantly with the motivation of care. I consider how care might be motivated by elaborating Iris Murdoch's vision metaphor to show that care is developed through regular attention to exemplary objects and events.

As well as relying on Murdoch's metaphor of attention, there are other insights from her short book *The Sovereignty of Good* which have informed my work. Murdoch writes that: "The unexamined life can be virtuous. . . . It must be possible to do justice . . . [to] the virtuous peasant."[6] Both a simple peasant and an intellectual can be caring. However, neither the expertise of a moral philosopher nor the innocence of a peasant is what is essential to care. What is distinctive about a caring person is the importance of other sentient beings to his or her life. It is clear, then, that this book, although explicating what is distinctive about a caring person, will not contribute to someone being a caring person. This is because to be caring is to be morally motivated. Education of a caring person consists primarily in motivating him or her to care. My purpose is to establish care as a certain type of motivation and to discuss how someone might become motivated to care.

Notes

1. Carol Gilligan, *In A Different Voice: Psychological Theory and Women's Development* (Cambridge: Harvard University Press, 1982).
2. Works directly inspired by Carol Gilligan's *In A Different Voice* include the following: *Social Research* 50 (1983) — special issue devoted to Carol Gilligan's *In A Different Voice; Signs: Journal of Women in Culture* 11 (1986) — "On *In A Different Voice:* An Interdisciplinary Forum"; and *Women and Moral Theory,* eds. Eva Feder Kittay and Diana T. Meyers (Totowa, N.J.: Rowman and Littlefield, 1987).

    Since the publication of *In A Different Voice,* there has been a proliferation of work on women and morality which, although not in direct response to Gilligan, is often inspired by this work.
3. Nel Noddings, *Care: A Feminine Approach to Ethics and Moral Education* (Berkeley: University of California Press, 1984).
4. I have found that attempting to use both feminine and masculine referents when discussing situations which pertain to both genders is confounded when quoting from material whose authors do not recognize the significance of exclusive use of masculine referents. Debating whether to alter someone's exclusive use of masculine referents by putting feminine or neutral words in brackets exemplifies the uncertainty a reader may experience when reading a work which uses only masculine referents. I have been unable to make the adjustments which I thought would reflect the moral lives of women and men because I was not sure whether particular writers meant their work to apply only to men.
5. For example, Nel Noddings reflects this difference by using feminine pronouns when referring to the "one-caring" in *Caring: A Feminine Approach to Ethics and Moral Education.*
6. Iris Murdoch, *The Sovereignty of Good* (London: Routledge and Kegan Paul, 1970), p. 2.

2

The Relationship of Care to Motivation

Such words as *ought, good, right,* and *care* have both moral and non-moral uses. Something may be aesthetically good, for example, or mathematically right, and I may be told that I ought to pick up my dry-cleaning by six o'clock. So too, I can care that my silverware is polished or care about my garden. *Prima facie,* none of these have moral implications. *Ought, good, right,* and *care* are part of the moral domain when reference is made to welfare and fair treatment of sentient beings. Care belongs to the moral domain when the object of care is someone or something whose welfare or fair treatment can be affected.

Simply put, to say that one cares that something is the case is to say that it matters or makes a difference to the person who cares that it is the case. Someone who cares that something is the case is motivated to have it, if possible, occur. You would have reason to doubt my sincerity if, given the opportunity, I did nothing to attempt to make something happen when I claim to care that it does happen. If I claim to care that my home is tidy but I never do anything to make it tidy, even when it is possible for me to do so, you have good reason to believe that a tidy home does not really matter to me. To care that something occur is to be motivated to bring it about, even though in some situations one may be unable to do so.[1]

Connected to caring "that" something occurs are the notions of caring "about" and caring "for". Caring "for" is a task-oriented concept which describes what might be involved in tending for someone or something else, whereas caring "about" is to acknowledge or pay attention to something. One can care for (tend to) someone or something and not care about the person or thing and one can care about someone or something and not care for (tend to) it. Those in the "helping" professions, for example, tend to (care for) others as part of their work responsibilities; they may not care about these people, although often they do. If one cares that another's welfare is enhanced, then one cares about the person. Conversely, if one cares about another, one is likely motivated to enhance the person's welfare, although not necessarily in every situation. Caring that someone's welfare is enhanced may or may not, however, result in caring for the person. This is because not all instances in which the welfare of a sentient being is at stake require that an individual be tended to (caring, for example, that someone returns safely from a trip does not). In those cases which do require that someone or something be cared for, it is not always necessary or possible for the person who cares to be the "caretaker." Someone in Canada, for example, may make it possible for a child in Ethiopia to be cared for by another.

Carefulness and carelessness refer to the degree of involvement someone has in a situation. It is unlikely that someone who cares that something occurs would be careless in attempting to bring about its occurrence. If someone is strongly motivated for something to occur, that person is likely to be careful. Someone is more likely to be careless if there is weak motivation that something occur.

What interests me in this book is understanding care as a motivational concept. Since ultimately my concern is to suggest ways in which care may, in turn, be motivated, it is important to be more clear about what is involved when someone cares that something occur.

Motivating and Justifying Reasons

I have said that, if someone cares that something occur, he or she is motivated to bring it about. To be motivated to bring something about, one must have certain beliefs about the context in which one is to act and beliefs about what would be required to have a particular situation occur. One must also have an ability to recognize a particular situation as an instance which fits into a particular context. For example, if I want to have money from my bank account when the bank is closed, I must have beliefs about bank cards and bank machines and I must be able to recognize a situation as one in which it is appropriate for me to do a transaction involving bank cards and bank machines.

According to Don Locke,[2] in order to be motivated to act a person requires a set of second beliefs that, given a set of first beliefs, an action is the rational thing to do.[3] Locke rightly says that having only the beliefs, for example, that roses are red or that sugar is sweet is not sufficient to motivate someone to do anything.[4] The first belief must be accompanied by a second belief about the first belief which makes an action possible. Applied to the bank card example, Locke's claim would be: (1) first belief: I believe that by putting my bank card in the machine, I will receive money; (2) second belief: I believe that given my belief about my bank card and the machine, it is appropriate to put my bank card in the machine. Both these beliefs may be necessary for a response to occur, but Locke is incorrect to suggest that these beliefs are sufficient. I may, in fact, have both beliefs but not be motivated to act because I have, at this moment, a wallet full of money and do not want any more. It is only if I also desire to have money from the machine that I am motivated to put my bank card in the machine.[5]

In order to be motivated to respond, I must desire to respond to relevant beliefs about a situation. If I believe that putting my bank card in a bank machine will allow a transaction, then I have a reason for putting my bank card in the machine, but only if I also want to do a transaction. The belief that putting the card in the machine will allow a transaction is inert without a desire to do the transaction. Equally important, if I do not have a belief that putting my card in the machine will allow a transaction, a desire to do a transaction is also inert. A motivating reason to respond in a particular situation requires, then, both desire and beliefs if someone is to, in fact, respond.

Although they are not sufficient to motivate a response, beliefs about beliefs, as described by Locke, are necessary components of motivation. Beliefs about beliefs are appraisals or evaluations. To appraise is to "see" one's beliefs according to a particular description. I must see this as a situation in which it is appropriate to put my bank card in the bank machine otherwise my beliefs about banking and my desire to have money do not lead to a response.

Some beliefs about beliefs are beliefs about the context in which an action takes place. To have these beliefs about beliefs is to have an understanding of what justifies an action within an enterprise. An action to put a bank card in a bank machine is justified, for example, by the enterprise of banking; moving chess pieces in a prescribed way on a chess board is justified by the game of chess; and responding to someone who is injured is justified by the domain of morality. Just as other beliefs about beliefs are not sufficient to motivate action, beliefs about which actions are justified within an enterprise are not sufficient to motivate an action. Someone may, for example, understand that the action of jumping over a bar is justified by the enterprise of high jumping without being motivated to jump over a bar. So too, someone can understand that a particular action is justified because a situation is a moral situation without being motivated to do the action.

A distinction can be made, then, between reasons which justify and reasons which motivate. Someone must have an understanding of the context within which an action makes sense in order to respond within the context but reasons which justify actions as a particular type of action are not sufficient to motivate an action. For example, when Dr Alexander submits her grades to the registrar's office, this action is to be understood within the context of a university and in relation to the enterprise of evaluation. The reasons which justify submitting grades at a university give meaning or context to Dr Alexander's actions. This meaning is absent if she attempts to submit grades to her opponent while she is playing a chess game. The provision of reasons which justify an action in relation to the purpose of a university and the enterprise of evaluation do not, however, also motivate someone to submit grades. If Dr Alexander does not desire to submit her grades, justifying reasons are not sufficient to motivate her to do so.

Reasons which motivate consist of beliefs about the context within which a response is to occur, other relevant beliefs, and the person's desire with respect to these beliefs. Notwithstanding conflicting desires, motivating reasons are necessary and sufficient to motivate action. If someone has a motivating reason to respond, this person *cares* that he or she responds. Dr Alexander submits her marks when she has beliefs about recording student evaluations at a university and when she desires that evaluation of her students be recorded. This desire and her beliefs about recording evaluations at a university constitute her motivating reason for action. Moreover, if she desires to submit her marks based on these beliefs, she can be described as caring that her marks are submitted.

When attempting to explain someone's response, it is not always necessary to mention both desire and belief even though both are essential if a response is to occur. It is only necessary to mention both desire and belief in an explanation if the listener is not clear how either a belief or a desire alone explain a particular response. Often, an explanation may refer to neither desire nor belief, although they can be inferred from the explanation. If, for example, I am asked why I am running the tap water and I answer "to wash the dishes," the listener can infer that I desire to wash the dishes and that I believe that running the tap water will contribute to that action.

A motivating reason is neither necessary nor sufficient to explain all bodily movements. Both actions and bodily movements can be explained by mechanical and physiological descriptions. Motivating reasons apply only to actions. Being an agent is to have at least some of one's bodily movements capable of explanation by motivating reasons. Being an agent who responds *morally* is to have, as I will show, motivating reasons which are morally justifiable.

Character Traits

Someone may care that something occurs in a particular instance, but not care whether it or something like it occurs in other instances. For example, I may care that you not suffer as a result of a fall in the street, but I may not care whether you or others suffer in other circumstances in which you are hurt. Instances of periodic or isolated care can be distinguished from fairly permanent motivation by understanding the nature of character traits. I will initiate a discussion of character traits here and continue this discussion in more detail in the next chapter.

I want to argue that character traits are desires which someone has fairly permanently. Character traits apply to persons. A character trait is what a person is. This position needs to be defended against the view that character traits are merely consistent ways of behaving. William Alston[6] claims, for example, that character traits, unlike desires, are frequently manifested in behavior. According to Alston, to ascribe a character trait to someone is to indicate that this person is disposed to behave in a way correlated to the trait and that he or she behaves in this way relatively frequently:

> Unless P has obeyed some orders, it cannot be correct to call him obedient, unless P has actually shown appreciation, he could not be termed appreciative, unless he has conformed to social conventions, he is not conventional.[7]

Desires, on the other hand, says Alston, are not always manifested in behavior. One can, for example, desire to be liked but never do anything to get others to like you.[8] It is, however, because character traits *are* desires that they do, in fact, have the features that Alston ascribes to desires. As desires, character traits are not always manifested in behavior. For instance, we do not refrain from calling an individual courageous who is presented with only one opportunity to save others; nor do we necessarily withhold ascribing this character trait after only one instance of courageousness.[9] Furthermore, as I discuss more fully in chapter 4, an accounting of behavior is not adequate as an assessment of how someone actually responds. Someone who is unable to do anything to assist another in a burning building, for example, may still be caring. On the other hand, someone assisting an individual who has fallen in the street may be a caring person, but it is also possible that this person is someone who hopes to be rewarded for assisting. Behavior alone does not reveal the motivation with which someone responds.

Alston claims that the behavior to which a character trait is ascribed can be explained by a number of different motives. According to him, a given trait is not identified with any particular desire; a given trait may be manifested for very different motives. As an example, he claims that, although we may indicate that certain actions of someone are polite actions, and, therefore, that this person is a polite person, "we are inclined to say that the fact that he is a polite person doesn't *really* explain *why* he acts politely in a particular case."[10] This person could want to ingratiate himself, for example.

Contrary to Alston, kind behavior, for example, cannot be explained by a number of different motives. Rather, if someone is kind, kind behavior can be manifested in a myriad of ways. If we know that someone's frequent actions of assistance and words of assurance are done in order to improve his or her own status or well-being, we do not commonly refer to this person as being kind. Actions alone do not establish kindness. The actions must be done from a desire to assist.

Not all ascriptions of desires attribute character traits to people. Desires which have a "satiation phenomenon"[11] are not character traits. Desire for water, for example, is satiated after consuming a certain amount of water, but a desire that others not suffer is not satiated after coming to the aid of a few suffering people. A desire for chocolate cake is satiable; a desire for fair treatment is not.

Not all ascriptions of people attribute desires to them. When we indicate that someone is cheerful or excitable, for example, we are not saying that this person has a desire. These "stylistic traits"[12] merely affirm that a corresponding form of behavior has occurred relatively frequently in the past. Stylistic traits such as cheerfulness, conceit, and excitability do not have an end to which they are directed. If one desires, one must desire something. When someone has the character trait of benevolence, or honesty, or courage, this person desires a particular end and does so fairly permanently.[13] (I will say more about this in the next chapter.) When one is timid, sarcastic, skeptical, and so on, one exhibits only a certain style.

Justifying Morality

In the chapters which follow, I will be more specific about the characteristics of moral care as well as suggest some ways that moral care can be developed in a person. As suggested by some psychological literature, moral care may have its basis in empathetic distress which is a response to the misfortunes of others found in very young children. Although empathetic distress may be the basis of moral care ("because its occurrence shows that we may involuntarily and forcefully experience others' emotional states rather than only the emotional states pertinent and appropriate to our own situation [and] . . . that . . . distress will often be contingent not on our own, but on someone else's painful experience",[14] it is important to understand that occurrence of empathetic distress as a natural condition does not provide *justification* for the development of empathetic distress. Young children also demonstrate aggressive behavior toward others. We do not think that this, then, justifies the development of aggressive behavior. Despite the behaviors children do display, behaviors which are thought to be desirable must be justified on grounds independent of the fact that they are displayed early in a child's life.[15]

The development of empathy can be justified on moral grounds. If someone asks for justification of morality, an answer would make some reference to the importance of minimizing suffering and enhancing welfare and fair treatment. If this person then asks, "Why should I want that?", there is no further answer which can be given. Stephen Toulmin calls a question of this kind a "limiting question" because, as he says, "I could only reply by asking in return, 'What better kinds of reason could you want?' "[16] If someone asks this "limiting" question, this person is asking for a reason why he or she should be motivated by this reason which justifies morality. When I referred to justification earlier, it was with respect to the ways in which certain actions are justified as part of a particular enterprise. For example, helping actions are justified by the enterprise of morality. In this instance, I am referring to the justification of morality itself. If reasons which justify treating someone well and fairly do not already count with someone, provision of reasons which justify morality are unlikely to convince this person to be moral. It is contradictory to give someone self-interested reasons to be moral. But one also cannot provide moral reasons to a self-interested person to be moral since moral reasons do not motivate this person.[17] If, for example, someone asks for reasons why he shouldn't tell a blind vendor that he has given her a ten dollar bill when he has actually given her a one dollar bill, moral reasons would refer to how this deception harms the vendor. If the customer asks why that should matter to him, an embellishment of reasons which justify morality won't help because these reasons don't count for this person. But to say something like, "you should not deceive the vendor because all transactions are being videotaped," is to give a reason not to deceive the vendor which is in the customer's self-interest. To abstain from deception for this reason would not be moral behavior.

As Rodger Beehler says, "only *some kinds* of reasons, only *some kinds* of considerations are moral reasons. . . . Of course, if one doesn't find these reasons compelling, well, one doesn't. But this does not make the reasons one does find compelling *moral* reasons — by default. . . ."[18] How is a person compelled or motivated by *moral* reasons? How does someone come to care that others are treated well and fairly? I will address the

13

question about motivation of care later, but I must first say something more about the moral domain and the fairly permanent desires some people have that welfare and fair treatment of others is enhanced.

Notes

1. Since care entails motivation for action, as a moral concept it is different from David Hume's sympathy. Annette Baier writes that morality for Hume "rests ultimately on sentiment, on a special motivating feeling we come to have once we have exercised our capacity for sympathy for others' feelings. . . ." ("Hume, the Women's Moral Theorist?" in *Women and Moral Theory*, edited by Eva Feder Kittay and Diana T. Meyers (Totowa, N.J.: Rowman and Littlefield, 1987), p. 41. This "motivating feeling" is not motivation for action. It is a passive evaluation by a spectator of another's qualities or characteristics. According to Hume:

   "My sympathy with another may give me the sentiment of pain and disapprobation, when any object is presented, that has a tendency to give him uneasiness; though I may not be willing to sacrifice anything of my own interest, or cross any of my passions, for his satisfaction."
   A Treatise of Human Nature, edited by L. A. Selby-Bigge, 2nd ed. (Oxford: Clarendon Press, 1888), p. 586.

2. Don Locke, "Beliefs, Desires and Reasons for Action," *American Philosophical Quarterly* 19 (1982): 243.

3. Locke, p. 247. There is an important truth in what Locke says about beliefs. It is not adequate merely to have a belief; one must also acknowledge or spell out to oneself the significance of the belief to one's actions. To do otherwise, as Herbert Fingarette suggests in *Self-Deception* (London: Routledge and Kegan Paul, 1969), is to risk self-deception.

4. Locke, p. 242.

5. Desire to have money from the machine and beliefs about how to do such a transaction do not necessitate that I will put my card in the machine. Although people often have certain relevant beliefs and desires, they may not act because of conflicting desires which are stronger.

6. William Alston, "Toward a Logical Geography of Personality Traits and Deeper Lying Personality Characteristics," in *Mind, Science and History*, eds. H. E. Keifer and M. K. Munitz (Albany: State University of New York Press, 1970), pp. 59-92.

7. Alston, p. 62.

8. Alston, p. 62.

9. Richard Brandt, "Traits of Character: A Conceptual Analysis," *American Philosophical Quarterly* 7 (1970): 26.

10. Alston, "Toward a Logical Geography of Personality Traits," p. 87.

11. Brandt, "Traits of Character: A Conceptual Analysis," p. 29.

12. Brandt, p. 27.

13. See Richard Brandt's "Traits of Character: A Conceptual Analysis" for an excellent discussion of character traits as fairly permanent motivation. Brandt argues that a character trait is a desire, an aversion, or an absence of desire. Courage, for example, "is essentially the absence . . . of an all-absorbing

attachment to personal safety and position" (p. 35). In other words, courage is the absence of a desire to avoid any risk to one's safety and position.

14. Martin Hoffman, "Empathy, Role-Taking, Guilt, and Development of Altruistic Motives," in *Moral Development and Behavior,* ed. Thomas Lickman (New York: Holt, Rinehart and Winston, 1976), p. 126.
15. Steven Gould writes in *Ever Since Darwin* (New York: Norton, 1977), p. 257:
    Why imagine that specific genes for aggression, dominance, or spite have any importance when we know that the brain's enormous flexibility permits us to be aggressive or peaceful, dominant or submissive, spiteful or generous? Violence, sexism, and general nastiness *are* biological since they represent one possible subset of a possible range of behaviors. But peacefulness, equality, and kindness are just as biological — and we may see their influence increase if we can create social structures that permit them to flourish.
16. Stephen Toulmin, *An Examination of the Place of Reason in Ethics* (Cambridge: At the University Press, 1972), p. 86.
17. I am aware that reference to self and others may reinforce another dichotomy. See, for example, Caroline Whitbeck, "A Different Reality: Feminist Ontology," in *Beyond Domination: New Perspectives on Women and Philosophy* (Totowa, New Jersey: Rowman and Allanheld, 1984). Whitbeck writes:
    One becomes a person in and through relationships with other people; being a person requires that one have a history of relationships with other people and the realization of the self can be achieved only in and through relationships and practices. (p. 82)
    See also Annette Baier, *Postures of the Mind: Essays on Mind and Morals* (Minneapolis: University of Minnesota Press, 1985). For example:
    Persons are essentially successors, heirs to other persons who formed and cared for them, and their personality is revealed both in their relation to others in response to their own recognized genesis. (p. 85)
    Although a notion of self which acknowledges the necessary connection to others is an insight which in important ways eliminates a self-others dichotomy, it is still necessary to have language which will account for the person who, nevertheless, sees himself or herself as autonomous and is motivated to act primarily for this self.
    I also do not wish to imply that acting for oneself in a moral situation is necessarily to act immorally. Clearly, a moral agent is also a sentient being and there will be occasions in which it will be important to take account of one's own welfare and fair treatment. It is particularly important, as I will show in chapter 5, that women see acting for themselves as legitimate in some moral situations.
18. Rodger Beehler, *Moral Life* (Oxford: Basil Blackwell, 1977), p. 60.

3

The Relationship of Care to Benevolence and Justice

A caring person is confronted with two different moral situations. There are those situations in which others are, for example, injured, starved, homeless, distraught, lost, confused, tormented, and the like — or in which, there is an opportunity for others to flourish. In this type of moral situation, welfare of others is at stake as a result of some predicament or circumstance which does not require a process of adjudication in order for welfare to be enhanced. When a caring person is confronted with this type of situation, his or her desire for the welfare of those in the situation is either a desire to help or (if not in a position to help) a desire that someone helps. This desire for others' welfare is a benevolent desire.

The other type of moral situation is one in which there is a conflict between sentient beings or between sentient beings and a standard, and the resolution requires adjudication so that those in the conflict are treated fairly. When a caring person is confronted with this type of situation, his or her desire that those in the conflict are treated fairly is either a desire to be fair (if he or she is an adjudicator) or a desire that others are fair as adjudictors. A desire for fair treatment of others is a just desire.

As a social being, a caring person is confronted with both moral situations. What is desired by a caring person in situations requiring adjudication is different from what is desired in situations not requiring adjudication because the general features of each type of situation are different. The object of a benevolent desire is welfare of those in a predicament or circumstance; the object of a just desire is the fair treatment of those in a conflict. In both instances, however, a caring person is motivated by what happens to sentient beings. If I care about a person or an animal, then I care that this being is treated well and fairly.

A caring person is motivated by welfare and fair treatment of those in a moral situation and not, for example, by any of the following:

1. a desire to be helpful to others so that they will reciprocate (do unto others as you would have them do unto you).
2. a desire to be rewarded (or not punished) by God, the state, the school, or other authorities.
3. a desire to uphold one's own integrity.
4. a desire to be a virtuous person.
5. a desire to uphold moral principles.

Behavior alone does not determine whether someone is a caring person. Often, behavior does not reveal an individual's motivation. Someone assisting another who has fallen in the street, for example, may be a caring person, but this person could instead hope to be rewarded for "helping." A caring person responds to someone who falls in the street because it is understood that another's welfare has been affected *and* because he or she is motivated to help another who has fallen. A self-interested person may also see that someone is in a predicament, see an opportunity to profit, and be motivated by this.

In examples one to four above, motivation is focussed on the agent and not on a possible recipient of the agent's response. In the first of these examples, an agent responds to another because he or she believes that to "help" others will ultimately be of personal benefit. Rather than being motivated to act because another is being harmed or treated unfairly, this person is motivated to "help" because to do so will pay off (honesty pays; honesty is the best policy). Notwithstanding that this belief assumes a great deal about how people respond to being treated well or fairly, the focus of a desire to respond is on self and not on the well-being of those in a particular moral situation.

In the second example, the agent acts to "help" others, not because those in a moral situation need help but because of a belief that if there is no action, opportunities to be rewarded will be missed or because of a belief that there will be unpleasant personal consequences (not going to Heaven, going to jail, being expelled from school).

Because examples three and four make reference to integrity and virtue (both of which have moral implications), these are often thought to be legitimate motivations for a caring person. It is clear, however, that the focus of motivation in these examples is not on a potential recipient of care. When someone responds in order to uphold his or her integrity or virtue, focus is only indirectly, if at all, on those whose welfare or fair treatment is at stake. In his book, *The Moral Life*, Rodger Beehler writes about the inadequacy of acting only from concern about "some 'moral state' of oneself." When this is one's motivation for acting, says Beehler, others are "simply occasions for 'moral' action." If one's concern is merely to be a "certain sort of person," this is not a moral concern since a moral concern is one which has "concern for other persons . . . at its heart."[1] And, as Lawrence Blum says in *Friendship, Altruism, and Morality*, if someone acts for the sake of virtue or for the sake of compassion, this person does not act from the "genuinely altruistic concern that compassion requires" for "it is not such a large step from acting for the sake of compassion to acting in order to maintain one's image of oneself as compassionate (and from there perhaps to acting in order to maintain others' image of oneself as compassionate)."[2]

The fifth motivation in the list refers to responding to those in moral situations because of a desire to fulfill moral principles. To be motivated to fulfill moral principles is not to focus on one's self, but it is not to focus on those in a moral situation either. Just how being motivated to fulfill principles relates to a caring response will be made more clear at the end of this chapter.

Care as a Benevolent Desire

If a person is caring, he or she will have a benevolent desire that others' welfare is enhanced in situations which do not require adjudication. This desire is either a desire to help personally or a desire that someone in a better position to help will help. If someone falls in the street, for example, a caring person has beliefs about such situations, including the belief that people who fall are often injured and that injured people ought to be helped. Moreover, a caring person desires that a particular injured person be helped. A caring person's motivating reason to help consists of these beliefs and a desire that another be helped. If a caring person is in a position to help, this person will desire to help, unless he or she has conflicting desires which are stronger than a benevolent desire to help.

A desire for someone's welfare in some situations may be a desire that welfare is enhanced, or in other situations it may be a desire that welfare is not diminished. A caring person may, for example, desire that another who presently lives in peace and in comfort continues to do so.

In some moral situations, a desire for the welfare of others is a desire that they flourish. A desire that someone flourish is a general desire that a caring person has for all sentient beings. But one can only have a specific desire that a specific person flourish if one knows what counts as flourishing for that individual. To desire that a specific individual flourishes is dependent on knowing something about that individual. Less information is needed to know what counts as *suffering* for another sentient being because we share with others the potential to suffer. We do not, however, share particular life circumstances. Because of this, it is often difficult to desire (except in a general way) flourishing for others whose circumstances are unlike our own and whose interests and needs are not clear. I will have something more to say in chapter 4 about how care is necessarily different between friends and strangers as a result of knowing what counts as flourishing for a friend.

I have said that a desire for another's welfare is often a desire that the other is helped. Because one cannot possibly be in a position to help everyone who requires help, a desire for others' welfare must also necessarily consist of a desire that, when confronted with such situations, other people help those who need help. This, in turn, implies that a caring person cannot be indifferent to whether others will help. Since a caring person cares that others are helped but cannot help everyone, he or she necessarily has a commitment to changing both social structures and people so that others can be helped. A caring person cannot limit care to those actual moral situations in which he or she is involved. If someone does care that others' welfare is enhanced, a commitment to social change is required as well. It is essential that a caring person share the world with other caring people if others are to be helped and treated fairly and (also of importance) if caring people are not to be taken advantage of. In other words, there is a sense in which care must be reciprocal. As Seyla Benhabib writes: "The existence of ongoing social relations in a human community entails some definition of reciprocity in the actions, expectations, and claims of the group."[3] My point is that caring must be shared by those in a community because it is necessary to prevent some members of the community sacrificing their lives for other members and because welfare and fair treatment of some in the community cannot be achieved unless care for them is shared by others in the community.

Care as a Just Desire

A benevolent desire is directed at the welfare of others in those moral situations which do not require adjudication. A just desire is directed at fair treatment of others in situations in which adjudication is required to sort out conflicts either between sentient beings or between sentient beings and a standard of some kind.[4] A desire for fair treatment is a desire that others be treated fairly both in situations in which oneself is the adjudicator and in situations in which others adjudicate. Because a caring person cares that others are treated fairly (and not only in situations in which he or she is the adjudicator), boundaries of justice for a caring person extend beyond periodic instances in which he or she is called upon to make decisions to settle conflicts. A caring person is committed to conserving those institutions which function to treat others fairly; as well, a caring person is committed to change when change is necessary to achieve fair treatment in situations in which fairness has traditionally and systematically been denied.

A caring person who adjudicates a conflict is able to focus on those in a moral situation while being impartial to irrelevant personal features. Just what features of a person are irrelevant to an adjudication is not always obvious. Excluding someone from a public swimming pool because of race is clearly irrelevant to being able to enjoy swimming. Race is not always irrelevant, however. Because we live in a society in which race has often been used by adjudicators to exclude people, it follows that to be blind to race would be to favor those who have benefitted from racial exclusion. Personal features such as race, gender, class, and disability are far from being irrelevant in decisions in which bias toward people with certain features is either blatant or hidden. In many situations, to ignore these features is to interpret fairness as meaning that certain favored groups in a society should receive more.[5] Knowing when race, gender, class, and disability are relevant depends on being sensitive to how fairness might be affected if one takes account of past injustices. One must be able to ask oneself: "Is gender [race, class, disability] operative here? How is gender [race, class, disability] operative? What other effects do our strategies for eliminating . . . bias have?"[6] To recommend completely impartial adjudication of a conflict is to recommend a process so abstract as to be both impossible and unfair. To ignore distinguishing features is to see everyone as a generalized other rather than as a particular, concrete other with a concrete identity; consequently, to be impartial in this way is to risk being guilty of injustice.

It is possible, however, for someone to desire fair treatment for particular people in a conflict *and* not be influenced by personal preferences and attachments to these people when making a decision. To treat others fairly, both in one's institutional roles and in any informal role one has as an arbitrator in disagreements involving friends and family, is to be partial toward those in a conflict *qua* sentient beings. But this is not a partiality toward irrelevant personal features or to one's own relationships to these people: it is a partiality which reflects connections to others who are affected by conflict. Someone who connects to others is likely to reflect this "partiality" in the reasons which are provided to adjudicate a particular conflict. These relevant reasons are more likely to reflect interconnections than those reasons provided by an adjudicator who is not partial to the effects on others who are involved in conflict. I have more to say about this when discussing Carol Gilligan's work in chapter 5.

A caring person does not have to be aloof from the context of a moral situation in order to make a decision about it. Indeed, the significance of a moral response will depend upon the actual desires that the moral agent has for those *qua* others in a moral situation. Impartiality does not demand indifference. Impartiality does demand, however, that reasons for adjudicating a conflict are not personally beneficial. Iris Murdoch describes this ability as "detachment" — an ability to look at and love something without seizing, using, or appropriating it to the "greedy organism of the self."[7]

Being partial to others as sentient beings while being impartial to features which are irrelevant to the resolution of a conflict can be complex, particularly if one of those in the conflict is a friend or family member or if the conflict involves an animal.[8]

The process is difficult when a friend is involved because one is motivated to respond to a friend "precisely because he is one's friend."[9] But in conflicts involving a friend, it would be unfair to act for one's friend for no other reason than this person is one's friend. When one fulfills an institutional role, the interests of everyone in a conflict, including friends, must be treated impartially. It is not fair to select a family member to a position within an institution by virtue of that relationship. Since people often have difficulty being impartial toward family and friends, or because it is perceived that they would have difficulty being impartial, formal adjudicators are usually expected to withdraw when friends or family members are involved in conflicts which would normally be adjudicated by them. However, withdrawing from formal adjudicating roles will not exempt someone from having to adjudicate conflicts involving friends and family. There are many informal situations which involve friends and family members in conflicts, and these need to be adjudicated in a fair way.

One must be impartial between two people only if there is an actual conflict between them. It is not a violation of impartiality if I decide to, for example, cheer up a friend instead of a stranger, since there is not an actual conflict between a friend and a stranger in this type of situation. Everyone can always be helped in some way. When I decide to cheer up a friend, I do not decide to do so instead of cheering up a stranger. I do not know what counts as "cheering up" for a stranger. If I did, the person would not be a stranger. If I do not attempt to make everyone my friend, I do not cease to be impartial, because it is practically impossible for everyone to be my friend.

Whereas there is a tendency to discard impartiality when a conflict involves a friend, there is a tendency to neglect all of the important personal features of animals when a conflict involves an animal. This is particularly so when a social contract is thought to be the paradigm of justice. As John Rawls writes: the limits of a theory of justice are that "no account can be given of right conduct in regard to animals and the rest of nature."[10] When justice is thought to occur only as a result of a social contract which is formulated through rational verbal exchange, justice does not extend to animals. But, as Jeremy Bentham wrote:

> . . . a full grown horse or dog is beyond comparison a more rational, as well as a more conversable animal, than an infant of a day or week, or even of a month, old. But suppose they were otherwise, what would it avail? The question is not, Can they *reason?* nor, Can they *talk?*, but Can they *suffer?*[11]

In a conflict between non-human sentient beings and human sentient beings, fair treatment would entail that both are assisted according to the type of life appropriate to each. Mary Midgley says: "Overlooking somebody's race is entirely sensible. Overlooking their species is a supercilious insult. It is no privilege, but a misfortune, for a gorilla or a chimpanzee to be removed from its forest and its relatives and brought up alone among humans to be given what those humans regard as an education."[12] It is important, therefore, to assess just what a legitimate conflict between animals and humans is and, therefore, just what features of animals we must be partial to. As Midgley argues, it is reasonable to work out our decisions in conflicts between animals or between humans and animals based on the supposition that suffering and enjoyment increase as nervous systems grow progressively more complex.[13] If this is the only criterion, however, conflicts between humans and animals will always be resolved in favor of humans, including the decision whether to sacrifice animals in order to determine the chemical effects of human cosmetics or the effects of high speed car crashes. Arguably, conflicts of this type between animals and humans are not legitimate conflicts at all. There is no conflict between humans and orangutans as to which will be educated in the arts. And if there is a conflict between humans and orangutans about which should predominate in the rain forests, fair treatment would likely favor the orangutans.

Adjudication of a conflict may result in enhancement of welfare. Often, however, adjudication will result in diminished welfare for one or more in a conflict, even though fair treatment is achieved for all. If, for example, a students is denied her university degree because her grades have not been accurately recorded by the registrar's office, fair adjudication of the problem would result in her obtaining credit for her courses and being awarded her degree. This would also enhance her welfare.[14] But when two people conflict over a parking spot, fair adjudication may result in one person losing any claim to the parking spot. They can both be treated fairly even though one's welfare is decreased as a result of having to look for another parking spot.

It is not fair if a benevolent desire overrides in a situation requiring that an adjucation be made even though those in the situation may not be treated benevolently. It is inappropriate for a benevolent desire to override in situations requiring justice, but it is nonsensical to have a just desire override a benevolent desire in a situation in which there is no adjudication. For example, if someone is sick in hospital, a caring person desires that this person recover. Unless there is some reason to believe that the sick person is not receiving attention commensurate with his or her illness, there is no need to desire the sick person's fair treatment.

Recognizing that situations differ according to certain important features is not to claim further that moral situations can be interpreted any way one wishes. On the contrary, features of moral situations are conceptually connected to what makes either a benevolent or a just desire appropriate as a motivation for a particular situation. Someone cannot simply decide that benevolence and not justice is more important in a situation in which, for example, one must adjudicate between two people getting into graduate school. One can, of course, be mistaken about the sort of situation it is, but one cannot simply decide that fair treatment of others is not at issue in this type of situation any more than one can decide to be kind to a utensil. There are no situations in which benevolence is more important than justice when a situation requires adjudication, and there are no instances in which justice is more important than benevolence in situations not requiring adjudication.

Benevolence and justice are each appropriate for different moral situations and, consequently, one cannot decide to make benevolence or justice more important in situations which do not have the relevant features. On occasion, however, when each demands a response at the same time, one may have to choose between responding to a situation for which benevolence is appropriate or responding to a situation for which justice is appropriate. In conflicts of this kind, one must consider the ways in which those in each situation will be affected by a decision to respond to the one situation and not to the other. As I will elaborate in the next chapter, if one desires to respond to both situations but can only act in one, there is still a response to both as long as there is a desire to act in both.

Benevolence and Justice as Character Traits

In chapter 2, I argued that character traits are fairly permanent desires which are not satiated after a few instances of acting on them. A caring person is someone who fairly permanently desires others' welfare and fair treatment. A caring person is benevolent and just — or, in other words, a caring person is someone who has the character traits of benevolence and justice.

Although I have referred to specific situations in which either a benevolent or a just desire is appropriate, the fact that a caring person fairly permanently desires others' welfare and fair treatment suggests that care is not limited to isolated instances. Caring is what someone *is*. This characteristic goes beyond particular moral situations. Because a caring person has fairly permanent benevolent and just desires, it is possible to say (as Iris Murdoch does) that moral life goes on continuously and is not switched off between explicit moral choices.[15]

Our lives are affected by events other than moral situations, and to claim that moral situations are to be found at every turn is to trivialize what actually affects sentient beings' welfare and fair treatment. It is morally trivial, for example, to avoid playing tennis because one will have to deceive one's opponent into thinking that one is going to lob the ball rather than drive it. To see every event in life as a moral situation would be to create difficulties where none exist. Action would be impossible because any action one took could adversely affect someone else. One would be forced to do nothing. For example, I may decide against getting on the bus because I might occupy the spot of someone else who wants to get on at a later stop. To react to every event as if it is a moral situation is also to deny the value of many non-moral attributes and events. As Susan Wolf says, when considering the characteristics of an ideal person: "one would hope that they would be morally good . . . but one would hope, too, that they are not *just* morally good, but talented, or accomplished or attractive in non-moral ways as well."[16]

The point I wish to make about the continuity of moral life is that there is consistency about the way caring people respond in moral situations because caring people have certain character traits. This is an important point because consistency is often thought to be characteristic of principles which are universal and not of desires which are often portrayed as fleeting and not dependable.[17]

In the previous chapter, I said that determination of whether someone has either a particular desire or a fairly permanent desire (character trait) cannot be ascertained by observing behavior alone because behavior does not indicate what motivates someone to act in the way he or she does. Moreover, some character traits — for example, courage — may be displayed infrequently because an individual may be confronted with few instances in which to display this character trait. It would be unusual, however, if a person had only a few opportunities to display benevolence or justice. Most people live in a social environment in which there are many

25

occasions to respond to others in moral predicaments. One could, of course, live in a monastery and, by so doing, remove both the opportunity to be morally compromised and the opportunity to respond benevolently or justly. Responding only to those moral situations with which one is occasionally confronted is inadequate if one is to be a caring person. Caring people do not merely wait for moral situations to come to them. If social structures prevent welfare or fair treatment from being achieved or if other people are too self-centred or unskilled to act, then a caring person is concerned that social structures and other people change.

Benevolence and Justice as Principles

Traditionally a contrast is made in philosophy between ethics as character or virtue and ethics as the dutiful application of principles. I argue that the morality of duty and the morality of character are complementary[18] and in such a way that duty complements character.

Although there are situations in which to act from duty is less morally significant than to act directly, it does not follow that to act from duty is "morally repugnant."[19] There are times when people must act from duty if they are to act at all. Acting from duty in these situations is the most morally significant way to act. However, acting from duty can, in certain situations, be morally repugnant.

> You are very bored and restless and at loose ends when Smith comes in once again. You are now convinced more than ever that he is a fine fellow and a real friend — taking so much time to cheer you up, travelling all the way across town, and so on. You are so effusive with your praise and thanks that he protests that he always tries to do what he thinks is his duty, what he thinks will be best. You at first think he is engaging in a polite form of self-deprecation, relieving the moral burden. But the more you two speak, the more it becomes clear that he was telling the literal truth: that it is not essentially because of you that he came to see you, not because you are friends, but because he thought it his duty, perhaps as a fellow Christian or Communist or whatever, or simply because he knows of no one more in need of cheering up and no one easier to cheer up.[20]

This strikes us as morally repugnant because there is someone who is supposedly a friend in the hospital and we think that the friend should be visited for that reason. Not all situations in which one acts from duty are as obviously this contrary to what someone who is caring would do. There are situations in which a caring person does not desire that a particular person in a moral situation is treated well or fairly. This may be because there is something particularly abhorrent about the person — for example, if the person is a child molester. Or, the caring person may have a conflicting desire the intensity of which is greater than a particular caring desire. If someone is caring, he or she recognizes that there is a principle which justifies responding to others who are in this type of situation and desires to perform a duty of benevolence or of justice. Actions may be identical, but in one instance the desire is directed at those in a moral situation and in the other instance the desire is directed at a recognized duty.

In what follows, I argue that a desire to perform a duty is less significant morally than a desire to respond directly to others in those situations in which it is possible to respond directly. In light of debate about the moral status of duty,[21] it is also important that I make clear how I see duty complementing character.

Duty of Benevolence

If someone *generally* cares that the welfare of others is enhanced and, as well, in a specific situation, desires a particular person's welfare, it is superfluous to indicate that he or she *ought* to desire the welfare of this person. A caring person already sees the point of caring and is motivated by this. It is not superfluous for a caring person to recognize an obligation when reflecting about a response, but this is not necessary at the time of the response.

From time to time, a caring person will be confronted with moral situations in which he or she does not specifically desire the welfare of those involved. When this happens, a caring person recognizes, nevertheless, that he or she has a duty to enhance the welfare of those in the situation. In these cases, if someone is caring, this person will desire to act on principles which justify acting benevolently in the particular situation. If, for example, Jones sees someone stranded at the side of the road as he is attempting to beat the rush-hour traffic, he may not have a particular desire to help the stranded stranger *qua* stranded stranger, but he may acknowledge that generally he believes that people should stop to help others in this type of situation. He recognizes that he has a duty to stop, and he desires to do his duty. He is a caring person because he fairly permanently desires others' welfare although, in this particular instance, he does not care whether the particular person is helped.[22]

Because the focus is on a duty to respond to reasons which justify benevolence in the situation rather than on those in the moral predicament, a dutiful response is less morally signficant than one directed at others. When one desires to do a duty, the focus is neither directly on others nor on oneself but on the principle which justifies helping those in a particular moral situation.

There is an important difference between acting because one desires to fulfill a principle and acting because one desires that others not suffer or be disappointed.

> I promise to meet you at the 5 o'clock train. You have checked the train schedules and determined that this is the train you can catch. I give you my word that I'll be there to pick you up. Now why ought I to keep my promise? . . . My failure to keep my promise leaves you standing on the station platform. By saying that I'll be there, I encourage you to rely on me to see to it that an interest of yours is met. By not keeping my promise, I let you down.[23]

To keep my promise because it is made to another person who is counting on me has more moral significance than to keep my promise because I recognize a duty to keep promises. As I have said, there are times when it is not possible to respond directly to others because of circumstance. In those situations, a dutiful response is not less morally signficant.

Duty of Justice

Just as one cannot have a specific benevolent desire for all sentient beings, it is not possible to have a specific desire that all others will always be treated fairly — one simply is not in a position to be aware of everyone who is treated unfairly. In some moral situations, it may be very difficult, even when one is aware of another, to desire fair treatment for this person. A caring person may, for example, not specifically desire that a morally repulsive person be treated fairly. In these instances, a caring person recognizes a duty to treat others fairly.

A caring person may, for example, be asked to adjudicate a conflict between a vendor who is known to exploit his workers and one of the workers who is the neighborhood bully. This caring person may have no particular just desire toward either of these people. However, because she does generally desire that others are treated fairly, she recognizes that she has a duty to be fair in this instance and she desires to fulfill this duty. The focus of her desire shifts from the people concerned to the duty itself. There is, then, only an indirect desire for the fair treatment of those in the conflict. A dutiful just response in this situation is less morally significant because it is possible directly to desire fair treatment for the vendor and the worker. In those situations in which it is not possible directly to desire another's fair treatment *qua* person, responding to duty is not less morally significant.

Conscientiousness

When a caring person does not specifically desire the welfare or fair treatment of those in a moral situation, this person desires to do a duty. This desire is conscientiousness. When someone responds conscientiously, the response is not the same as a direct response, even though the action may be the same. Moreover, assuming that it is possible to respond directly, the conscientious response is less morally significant. This view is contrary to that of W. D. Ross who claims that responding to duty is morally superior.

> Suppose that someone is drawn towards doing action A by a sense of duty and towards doing another, incompatable, act B by love for a particular person. *Ex hypothesi*, he thinks he will not be doing his duty in doing B. Can we possibly say that he will be acting better if he does what he thinks *is* his duty? . . . what is properly meant by the sense of duty is the thought that one *ought* to act in a certain way. . . . And it seems clear that when a genuine sense of duty is in conflict with any other motive we must recognize its precedence. If you seriously think that you ought to do A, you are bound to think you will be acting morally worse in doing anything else instead.[24]

Duty is morally significant in those situations in which a caring person does not specifically desire that those in a moral situation, *qua* sentient beings, are treated either well or fairly. But duty is less morally significant when it is possible to desire directly another's welfare or fair treatment.

> To see . . . conscientiousness as a substitute for . . . virtue brings out two important things. First, it indicates the absurdity of denying the value of that for which conscientiousness is a substitute. . . . Secondly, it shows that it is in its capacity to motivate a [person] to perform the same actions that a [person] with . . . [virtue] would be moved to do that the unique, though not supreme, value of conscientiousness lies.[25]

I will have more to say about the moral significance of moral responses in the next chapter, but for now it is worth looking at the type of situation suggested by Ross in which someone must decide whether to respond to a benevolent or just desire or to respond from duty. According to Ross's thinking, a desire to do one's duty would always take precedence over a desire to respond directly. My argument, however, is that if a duty takes precedence over a direct benevolent or just desire, it does not take precedence merely because it is a duty. If it takes precedence, it is because the features of the particular situation are such that the duty refers to principles which are pertinent. When, for example, a moral situation requires that an adjudication be made and someone desires the welfare of one person in the conflict to the detriment of others, recognizing a duty to be fair does take precedence over a direct desire to help one of those in the conflict. When a moral situation requires justice, the desire to do one's duty to be fair takes precedence over a benevolent desire to assist a particular individual. But if one has a direct desire to treat others fairly in a moral situation which requires adjudication, this desire takes precedence over a desire to do one's duty to treat an individual within the conflict benevolently. Acting on a desire to do one's duty to treat someone benevolently is appropriate only in situations in which no adjudication is required and is necessary only when one does not directly desire another's welfare.

In *Friendship, Altruism and Morality,* Lawrence Blum claims that conscientiousness and kindness "work in different areas of our lives."[26] Blum makes a distinction between kindness and conscientiousness whereas I make a distinction between benevolence and justice. Benevolence and justice "work in different areas of our lives" because the features of the situation for which each is appropriate are different. Someone can, however, be conscientious about both benevolence and justice when he or she does not have a specific benevolent or just desire in a particular moral situation.

Scope and Strength of Care

Any being who can feel and suffer is an object of care. The propensity to suffer is not limited to family and friends any more than it is limited to human beings. Mary Midgley argues against regarding the scope of morality as a series of concentric circles with oneself at the middle and working out to family, personal friends, age-group, colleagues, race, social class, nation, species, and the biosphere.[27] Those at the beginning of the list share the advantage of being close in time and space, but proximity is neither necessary nor sufficient for care to occur. I will have more to say about the scope of care when I comment about the relation of supererogation to care in chapter 4. Here, however, it is important to emphasize that a caring person is one who generally desires that other sentient beings are treated well and fairly. A caring person is not only moved by circumstances involving friends, family, or racial group, but also has fairly permanent desires that all sentient beings be treated well and fairly. As we will see in the next chapter, some of these circumstances are extraordinarily difficult. Just what a caring person does in a situation commonly thought to demand supererogatory action will become clear later.

Not only can care be understood with respect to its scope but also with respect to its intensity. Care can be strong or weak. I am not able to suggest what the threshold must be in order for care actually to be care, but it is clear that if either a benevolent or just desire is weaker in a particular moral situation than a conflicting desire, the conflicting desire will necessarily override. I may, for example, desire to assist someone who is lost, but if this desire is weaker than my desire to get to my next class, I will not respond. If a person's benevolent and just desires are always weaker than conflicting desires, the person is obviously not a caring person.

Notes

1. Rodger Beehler, *The Moral Life* (Oxford: Basil Blackwell, 1977), p. 31.
2. Lawrence Blum, *Friendship, Altruism and Morality* (London: Routledge and Kegan Paul, 1980), p. 100.
3. Seyla Benhabib, "The Generalized and the Concrete Other," in *Women and Moral Theory,* eds. Eva Feder Kittay and Diana T. Meyers (Totowa, New Jersey: Rowman and Littlefield, 1987), p. 175n. Benhabib's comment supports the work of Alvin Gouldner, "The Norm of Reciprocity: A Preliminary Statement," *American Sociological Review* 25 (1960): 161-78.
4. Joel Feinberg says in *Rights, Justice and the Bounds of Liberty: Essays in Social Philosophy* (Princeton: Princeton University Press, 1980), p. 266, that justice achieved when sentient beings conflict is comparative justice and justice which is determined independently of others is called non-comparative justice. Despite its name, non-comparative justice does involve a comparison but the comparison is with a standard.
5. Dale Spender, *Invisible Women: The Schooling Scandal* (London: Writers and Readers Publishing Cooperative Society, 1982), p. 55.
6. Barbara Houston, "Gender Freedom and the Subtleties of Sexist Education," *Educational Theory* 35 (1985): 368.
7. Iris Murdoch, *The Sovereignty of Good* (London: Routledge and Kegan Paul, 1970), p. 65.
8. There is a growing body of literature which indicates that adjudicators who have responsibility for choosing people to fill vacant positions choose people who resemble themselves. See, for example, Jeff Hearn and P. Wendy Parkin, "Gender and Organization: A Selective Review and Critique of A Neglected Area," *Organization Studies* 4 (1983): 219-42, and Rosabeth Moss Kanter, *Men and Women of the Corporation* (New York: Basic Books, 1977).
9. Blum, *Friendship, Altruism, and Morality*, p. 44.
10. John Rawls, *A Theory of Justice* (Cambridge: The Belknap Press of Harvard University, 1971), p. 512.
11. Jeremy Bentham, *An Introduction to the Principles of Morals and Legislation,* intro. Laurence J. Lafleur (New York: Hafner Publishing Co., 1948), p. 311n.
12. Mary Midgley, *Animals and Why They Matter* (New York: Penguin Books, 1983), p. 99. It may also be inappropriate to overlook someone's race at this point in our social evolution, since race has hitherto been used to exclude people.
13. Midgley, *Animals and Why They Matter*, p. 90.

14. This is an instance of a conflict between a sentient being and a standard. The standard is a set of accepted criteria for receiving a particular university degree.
15. Murdoch, *The Sovereignty of Good,* p. 37.
16. Susan Wolf, "Moral Saints," *The Journal of Philosophy* 77 (1982): 422.
17. Lawrence Blum writes in *Friendship, Altruism, and Morality:* ". . . let us consider a person who (*sic*) we would say is a sympathetic or compassionate person. Such a person would be prone to acting out of compassion or sympathy in certain situations (situations which 'warrant' sympathy or compassion). It seems that by saying that he is a compassionate or sympathetic person — in contrast to someone who is occasionally or inconstantly shows signs of compassion or sympathy — we are attributing a measure of consistency to his behavior." (p. 111)
18. William Frankena says in *Ethics,* 2nd ed. (Englewood Cliffs: Prentice-Hall, 1973), that, "I am inclined to think that principles without traits are impotent and traits without principles are blind" (p. 65).
19. Marcia Baron, "The Alleged Moral Repugnance of Acting from Duty," *The Journal of Philosophy* 63 (1976): 462.
20. Michael Stocker, "The Schizophrenia of Modern Ethical Theories," *The Journal of Philosophy* 63 (1976): 462.
21. See, for example, Michael Stocker, "The Schizophrenia of Modern Ethical Theories"; Bernard Williams, "Persons, Character and Morality," in *The Identities of Persons,* ed. Amelie Rorty (Berkeley, Ca.: University of California Press, 1976); Susan Wolf, "Moral Saints"; Marcia Baron, "The Alleged Moral Repugnance of Acting from Duty."
22. The importance of considering the social context of moral situations is clearly evident if the feminine pronoun is substituted in this example. It is not so clear that a woman in this circumstance has a duty to stop if the stranger is a man. I will say more about the effects of circumstance on a moral response in chapter 6.
23. Andrea Teuber, "Simone Weil: Equality as Compassion," *Philosophy and Phenomenological Research* 43 (1982): 229-30.
24. W. D. Ross, *The Right and the Good* (Oxford: Clarendon Press, 1930), p. 164.
25. Philip Mercer, *Sympathy and Ethics* (Oxford: At the Clarendon Press, 1972), p. 116.
26. Blum, *Friendship, Altruism and Morality,* p. 167.
27. Midgley, *Animals and Why They Matter,* p. 29.

4

 Caring Response

A caring person desires that changes are made in the lives of others so that, given the situation, they either receive fair treatment or their welfare is improved. A caring person may not actually be the one who acts to change another's circumstance. Often, as well, circumstances may not be subject to change. Even so, desiring that circumstances change for others is to respond to them. A benevolent or just desire is part of both the description of a caring person's motivation to respond in a moral situation and part of the description of the response itself.

Having only a desire to change another's circumstance without an attempt to do something will often be an inadequate response. In those moral situations in which an action is impossible, however, a desire that others' circumstances change is a morally significant desire. Someone who desires the welfare of another in an uncontrollable fire responds to this person even if the smoke and flames make it impossible to act. That this is so becomes more clear when someone who desires the welfare of another in a fire is contrasted to someone who watches the fire indifferently. Even though neither acts, the one who desires the welfare of the person in the fire responds to this person, and this response is morally significant even if there is no behavior possible.[1]

The nature of a response cannot be determined by behavior alone. If George visits Sam in the hospital, the nature of George's visit is different if he desires Sam's welfare than it is if he desires to do his duty or he has designs on Sam's fortune. Similarly, if Mary desires that Jane be treated fairly, this is a different response from Mary desiring to be ingratiated with Jane by ensuring that Jane receives fair treatment. To assess properly a response, it is necessary to know under what description the response is being considered.[2] George assisting Sam because it is in George's self-interest to help Sam is a different response from George assisting Sam because George desires Sam's welfare. The action and the motive for the action are both components of the description of a particular response. I return to this later.

I have argued that there are two basic moral situations: those which require adjudication of a conflict and those which do not because there is no conflict. I have also said that in each of these situations it is possible to respond to others either by directly desiring the welfare or fair treatment of those in a moral situation or by desiring to act from duty. It is possible, then, to identify four moral responses, two for each type of moral situation:

1) a response in which one has a direct desire for others' welfare in situations not requiring adjudication;
2) a response in which one has a desire to do one's duty in situations which do not require adjudication;
3) a response in which one has a direct desire that those in a conflict are treated fairly;
4) a response in which one has a desire to do one's duty in situations which involve conflict.

Each of these responses differs from the other by virtue of what the motivation for each is, as well as differences in specific behavior which may be appropriate for a particular moral situation. In what follows, I will show that each response is also distinguished by the type of reasons involved in each and by the role that emotions play in each.

Reasons

There are at least three kinds of moral reason all of which are important if one is to be a fully-functioning caring person. Each, however, has a different role in each of the four moral responses. Two of the three kinds of moral reason — moral motivating reasons and moral justifying reasons — were discussed in chapters 2 and 3. In the latter chapter, I introduced the notion of reasons to adjudicate conflicts. Here I will say something more about the relationship of moral adjudicating reasons to both the direct and the dutiful just responses.

Adjudicating reasons are reasons a caring person provides when adjudicating a conflict between sentient beings or sentient beings and a standard. A caring person adjudicates a conflict by providing relevant reasons why the conflict is adjudicated in the way that it is.[3] For example, in a dispute between a shopkeeper and a customer, a caring person desires the fair treatment of both people and, in order to treat them fairly, reasons relevant to the fair resolution of the conflict must be provided. While they may be relevant to the context of the situation (for example, hair color is not relevant to whether someone should be sold products at the same price as other people), reasons to adjudicate a conflict may emphasize either the separateness or the connectedness of people in a community. Adjudicating reasons which reflect connections between and among people may be an indication of someone's direct desire for fair treatment of those in a conflict, whereas adjudicating reasons which reflect separateness of those in a conflict may be an indication of acting from duty. I will return to this in chapter 5. Regardless, however, of whether one is motivated directly by those in a conflict or by duty, adjudicating reasons are essential to completion of a response which requires adjudication.

A caring person will have occasion to utilize all three types of moral reason according to features of the particular moral situation and according to whether his or her response is a direct or a dutiful response. The following example illustrates the way in which motivating reasons, justifying reasons, and adjudicating reasons may all be part of a single response:

> Karen has been asked by two waiters to settle a dispute about the distribution of tip money. Karen is not fond of either waiter because she suspects them of pilfering cutlery. Her first inclination is to settle the dispute by pulling straws. But because she is a generally caring person, she believes that she ought to be just in this dispute as well. She acknowledges that people ought to be treated fairly in these types of situation and, on the basis of reasons which justify treating these particular people fairly, she desires to fulfill a duty to treat the waiters fairly. This desire, together with relevant beliefs about the waiters' dispute, is Karen's motivating reason to respond. After weighing the evidence from each waiter, she adjudicates the dispute by providing reasons which will solve the problem fairly. The reasons she provides to settle the dispute are relevant and impartial with respect to personal features of the waiters.

Caring Emotions

I have said that emotion is an important part of a moral response. I want now to indicate why that is by showing that the type of emotion, if any, an individual experiences can be morally significant to the recipient of a moral response. Before I am able to establish this, I must first develop a conceptual understanding of what an emotion is.[4] I do this by discussing the following:

(1) the relationship of emotion to feelings;

(2) the relationship of emotion to behavior;
(3) the relationship of emotion to beliefs, appraisals, and desires
(4) the relationship of emotion to motivation.

The Relationship of Emotion to Feelings

Emotions are not identical to feelings, but feelings are experienced by someone who has an emotion. If, for example, I am anxious about someone driving through a storm, I experience certain sensations. If I regret having treated someone poorly, I experience other sensations. There are those who argue, however, that feeling is not a necessary part of an emotion.

> If P comes upon Q just as Q is setting fire to P's house, and P rushes at him in blind fury, it seems singularly inappropriate to insist that P must be having certain sensations. In fact P, in such circumstances, probably experiences no sensations of any kind, and yet he is undoubtedly extremely angry.[5]

It is possible that someone may not be aware of his or her feelings because of being intent on something else. P may not be aware of his feelings because his attention is directed at punishing Q. If, however, someone does not have any out-of-the-ordinary feelings, even if momentarily oblivious to them, that person does not experience an emotion.

Although an emotion is experienced as a feeling, an emotion cannot be reduced to the feeling involved in physiological or mental changes. I reject the view expressed by William James, for example, that "bodily changes follow directly the perception of the exciting fact, and . . . our feeling of the same changes as they occur IS the emotion."[6]

There are a number of reasons, both empirical and conceptual, why emotions and feelings are not identical. Experimental evidence shows that "the same visceral changes occur in very different emotional states and in non-emotional states."[7] Furthermore, it is possible to drug-induce feelings of anger or fear without someone actually being angry or fearful.

If emotions were reducible to characteristic feelings, it would not be possible to make the conceptual distinctions we do make between emotions which have very similar feelings. For example, the physiological or mental feelings associated with envy and jealousy do not differ much, if at all, and consequently it is not these *feelings* which distinguish envy from jealousy.

The Relationship of Emotion to Behavior

The reduction of emotion to certain types of behavior can also be dismissed on experiential and conceptual grounds. Emotions are not always expressed either facially or as overt actions. This is not to say that behavior may not be helpful in interpreting another's emotions. "*A fortiori* we would not believe that someone has a certain emotion if he has often acted in a way that is rationally incompatible with that emotion. . . . we do look upon behavior as an 'external' or public indicator of 'inner' or private states."[8] There is, however, no one set of behaviours or changes in facial expression which is indicative of a particular emotion.

> While an angry man *may* "pound the table, slam the door, or pick a fight", he may not. He may stand stock still, go red in the face, tense, purse his lips, and then go out with studied calm. In short it is an impossible programme to find a list of behavioral items, some or all of which must be present if the behavior in question is to be dubbed angry behavior.[9]

Emotions do not have characteristic behaviors. Some emotions — for example, wonder and grief — may have no other behavioral manifestation that quiescence.[10] It is clear, however, that a conceptual distinction can be made between wonder and grief even though their behavioral manifestations are the same.

There is, then, a difference between an experience of an emotion and its display. If someone is described as unemotional, this may indicate only that this person does not display emotion and not that he or she does not experience emotion. Someone may experience emotion and not display it either because of an ability to control its display or because of an inability to express it. In chapter 7, I will return to the importance of being able to both control and express moral emotions.

The Relationship of Emotion to Belief, Appraisal, and Desires

There is a formal relationship which occurs between a conceptual understanding of a particular emotion and its object. For example, the object of one's embarrassment is something which is awkward or unpleasant; the object of one's fear is something which is threatening. The existence of a formal relationship between an emotion and an object is, of course, not adequate for someone to experience an emotion. A person must also have relevant beliefs about an object and evaluate these beliefs in a certain way. For example, in order for Jane to be angry at her child for spilling his supper on the rug, Jane must believe that there is something spilled on the rug and she must believe that her child spilled it. She can be mistaken in her beliefs. She may believe that the child spilled the supper when, in fact, the cat did.

Not only must I have beliefs about a situation. My appraisal or evaluation of these beliefs will affect what emotion, if any, I experience. Ortega's description of four people by a dying man's bed is illustrative of the way in which different people experience different emotions in the same situation:[11] present are the man's wife, his doctor, a reporter, and a painter — there is a different "emotional distance between each person and the event they all witness."[12] The painter evaluates the situation as one which has a certain combination of spatial and optical components. The reporter evaluates the situation factually. The doctor evaluates the situation professionally. Only the wife evaluates the situation as one which someone who is dearly loved is about to die. She experiences intense emotion.

Different appraisals of the same beliefs result in different emotions. The "object" of fear, for example, is something which is threatening but only if one appraises a situation as being threatening. I may believe that there is a grizzly bear on the path, appraise the situation as challenging, and experience excitement rather than fear.[13]

> Emotions are not differentiated by means of the object or even the subject's factual beliefs about the object but by means of the subject's evaluative beliefs about the object. . . . For your emotion is, say, not one of embarrassment unless you evaluate or view the situation as awkward or unpleasant. If you were thick-skinned and did not mind in the least meeting people whom you have rejected or failed in some way, then you would not evaluate such meetings as awkward and unpleasant, and so would not be embarrassed in such situations.[14]

In order for Jane to be angry about the spilled supper, she must evaluate her beliefs about her child spilling his supper as disagreeable or thwarting. If she evaluates the same beliefs about the spilled supper as an indication of the child's independence, she may experience something like pride.

There are also different experiences of emotion depending upon what someone desires. Jane will experience pride in her evaluation of her child being independent, for example, only if she desires that the child be independent. If she does not desire this, she will experience something like annoyance.

Emotion is, then, a feeling one experiences when one has a particular desire, has beliefs about an object or event, and evaluates these beliefs in a certain way. I desire not to be harmed, and I believe that this is an animal with very sharp claws. If I also evaluate the animal as threatening, I experience *fear*. Fear is the feeling one experiences when one desires not be be harmed when evaluating something as threatening. This is not to say that all combinations of desires and beliefs have a corresponding emotion. They do not. But all emotions entail a corresponding desire and evaluated beliefs.

Because an emotion involves evaluation of beliefs, an emotion can sometimes be unreasonable. If an individual is afraid of a flower, for example, this does not indicate that all emotional experience is unreasonable. It does show instead that the individual experiences an unreasonable emotion. An unreasonable fear of a flower can be explained in the following ways:[15]

1. "[His] reason for being afraid is expressible in a statement, which, if true, would state a good reason for being afraid, but which is actually false and, in the given circumstances, obviously false. . . . (Baseless or unfounded fears)." It is unreasonable to be afraid of a flower because it is poisonous when it is obvious (to the person who is afraid) that the flower is a daisy.
2. "He acknowledges that there is no danger, and yet he is afraid. . . . (Irrational fear)." It is unreasonable to be afraid of a flower if one admits that the flower is harmless.
3. "His reason for being afraid, although expressed in a true statement, states an extremely bad reason, or what might be called 'no reason' for being afraid. . . . (Superstitious fear)." It is unreasonable to be afraid of a flower for the reason that anything that is placed on graves, including flowers, is to be avoided.
4. "The object of his fear is an unsuitable one . . . . (a vain or neurotic fear)." It is unreasonable to be afraid of a flower for the reason that flowers excrete pollen on one's clothes.
5. "The object of his fear is a suitable one, but his fear is too great. . . . (Abnormal or indiscriminate fear)." It is reasonable to fear poisonous flowers but not to the extent that one runs away even when seeing them in a glass display case.

Reasonable or unreasonable experience of emotions depends on the reasonableness of beliefs and the reasonableness of the evaluation of these beliefs. Emotions can also be displayed either reasonably or unreasonably. Reasonable display of emotions will be addressed in chapter 7.

The Relationship of Emotion to Motivation

Although commonly one says, for example, that I ran away because I was afraid, strictly speaking it is not emotion which prompts action but motivation. Emotion and motivation are not the same; emotions are conceptually linked to certain motivating reasons. R. S. Peters argues for a distinction between emotions and motives because, as he says, motives connect evaluations with action while emotions connect evaluations with things that come over us.[16] Emotions are passive, says Peters; the only actions initiated by emotions are involuntary — our knees knock, we perspire, we blush. I, too, argue that emotions and motives are different, but I also argue for a conceptual connection between emotions and the desires and beliefs which make up certain motivations. Some emotions are followed by action, but only if the desire to which it is connected leads to action. For example, I run away because I desire not to be harmed by the grizzly bear. Since I desire not to be harmed and I see a situation as one in which I will be harmed if I stay, I run. A desire not to be harmed and an evaluation of a situation as one in which I will be harmed also result in my experience of fear. It is not the feeling of fear which motivates me to run. I run because I do not want to be harmed by the bear. Emotions may affect the efficacy of an action, but emotions do not motivate actions. "My fear may lead me to use more (or less) force in applying the brakes, may increase (or decrease) my reaction time, or may lead me to think (or fail to think) of some useful strategem."[17]

Rather than see the relation between emotion and motivation as emotion leading to motivation (fear leading me to run away), it is essential to stress that the necessary relation between emotion and motivation is one in which an emotion is the necessary result of a particular desire and certain evaluated beliefs. William Lyons, for example, says that a person first has beliefs upon which he or she makes an evaluation which, in turn, causes the desire which leads to behavior.[18]

> To take a simple case of fear, the sight of a ferocious dog might cause Fred to evaluate it as threateningly dangerous to him such that he wants to run away and escape, and so he takes to his heels.[19]

Because Fred evaluates a dog to be threatening and he desires not to be hurt, he feels afraid. Beliefs, evaluation of those beliefs, and a desire not to be hurt are what motivate Fred to run away. He also experiences fear as a result of these conditions. And, of course, he may not run away if there is nowhere to run. Not all emotions are followed by action. Grief, for example, usually is not.

Because emotions are only linked to actions by way of desires, they appear to be superfluous.[20] But the importance of caring emotions does not depend on whether they motivate action. Caring emotions are important, as I argue next, because of their significance to others.

Caring Emotions

One of Kant's major objections to recognizing emotions as morally significant was that he thought emotions to be natural to some and not to others.

Consequently, he thought that this would make "the capacity for moral worth a species of natural advantage" which would be "both logically incompatible with the notion of *the moral*, and also in some ultimate sense hideously unfair."[21] Experience of a caring emotion is a necessary result of caring that someone is treated well or fairly. If a caring person desires another's welfare or fair treatment and this desire is either fulfilled or thwarted, this caring person will experience an emotion. If, for example, someone desires that another be treated fairly, has beliefs about what constitutes fair treatment in a particular instance, and evaluates the situation as one in which another is not treated fairly, this person will experience an emotion. If someone does not receive fair treatment when fair treatment is desired and the other conditions are met, a caring person will experience either disappointment or anger, depending on the severity of the situation. If the other person receives fair treatment, a caring person experiences either satisfaction or joy. Similarly, if someone desires another's welfare, has beliefs about what constitutes welfare in a particular situation, evaluates a situation as an instance in which another's welfare is at stake, and finds that no one is able to help, this person experiences regret or sorrow. If a caring person does not act because of a conflicting desire that is stronger than the desire for another's welfare, he or she experiences guilt or remorse. And so on.

Emotions such as sadness, anger, and joy are not only caring emotions but also, for example, aesthetic emotions or self-interested emotions. They are caring emotions only when they are the consequence of moral motivation. Emotions experienced as a result of being motivated by self-aggrandizement (for example, experiencing joy at receiving a benefit from someone's suffering) are not, of course, caring emotions, although they must be considered when accounting for caring emotions.[22] When a self-aggrandizing emotion is experienced in a moral situation, this emotion is an immoral emotion. In the final chapter, I will discuss educational implications of contending with immoral emotions.

A caring emotion is conceptually connected to moral motivating reasons; it is part of a caring response; and it is morally significant to a recipient of a response. A caring emotion is significant to a recipient because, if properly displayed, it is an indication that the person who responds actually desires the recipient's welfare or fair treatment. The sincere display of emotion indicates whether another's behavior is the result of motivation directed at another in a predicament or in a conflict. This is why, as I will comment in chapter 7, education of caring emotions consists both in development of caring motivation and development of appropriate emotional expression.

Some experience or display of emotion may, in fact, be detrimental to a caring response. If someone experiences extreme despair as a result of another's situation, the emotional experience, while morally significant, may be harmful if it incapacitates this person in fulfilling a role, say, as an adjudicator. An adjudicator who becomes overwhelmed by the plight of others in conflict situations may have an *ability* to adjudicate problems but be unable to shift attention from his or her emotional experience. Similarly, if someone has the ability to provide first aid to an accident victim but is overwhelmed by emotions and is unable to utilize these skills, the skills are useless. Neither excessive experience of emotion nor excessive display of emotion is an indication, however, that emotion should not be experienced or displayed. Someone is unjustified in his or her *experience* of emotion only if there is no justification for the desire and evaluated beliefs which are necessary for the emotion to occur.[23] A particular *display* of an emotion is unjustified when it inhibits action or does not sincerely convey caring desires to those in a moral situation.

I have said that there are occasions in which a caring person does not directly desire the welfare or fair treatment of those in a particular moral situation. Instead, this person desires to do a duty of benevolence or of justice. An experience of emotion by someone who desires that a duty be fulfilled is different from an experience of emotion by someone who directly desires the welfare or fair treatment of those in a moral situation. Someone who desires to fulfill a duty will experience either some degree of regret if thwarted in fulfilling this duty or some degree of satisfaction if the duty is fulfilled. There is, however, an important distinction between the emotional experiences in the two responses. Someone who desires the welfare or fair treatment of others will experience an emotion both during a moral situation and in response to the way in which the situation is resolved. This is because this person is motivated by what happens to those in the moral situation. If, on the other hand, I believe that I have a duty to help those stranded in a boat at sea and I am motivated by this duty, I will experience no emotion as a result of the predicament of those in the boat. I will feel unhappy if I think that I will not be able to fulfill my duty or, if the people in the boat return safely, I will experience satisfaction that I have fulfilled an acknowledged duty.

An emotion experienced as a result of a desire for others' welfare or fair treatment is significant to those in a moral situation because it is an indication of another's care for them *qua* people.[24] An emotion experienced as a result of a desire to fulfill a duty is not particularly significant to those in a moral situation because the emotion indicates no direct concern for those in the situation.

Caring emotions, although superfluous to action, are not superfluous to the significance of the total caring response. Since a caring response is not indicated by action alone, focus of motivation is central to whether emotional display is evidence of someone caring.[25]

Caring Responses

Throughout this work, I have argued against understanding morality solely through behavior. A caring response is not merely an action. In order to assess whether a response is a caring response, motivation must also be taken into account. Action is impossible in some moral situations, but someone responds in a morally significant way when desiring welfare or fair treatment of those in the situation. It is morally significant if someone desires to help someone who is drowning even if help cannot be provided.

In order for a response to be a caring response, it must be a response of someone who desires others' welfare or fair treatment — or, at least, it must be a response of someone who desires to fulfill a duty to others requiring welfare or fair treatment. Because of the conceptual connection between caring desires and emotion, a caring response will also be associated with an emotion at the time of a moral situation and/or upon recognition that one's desire has either been fulfilled or thwarted.

At the beginning of this chapter, four general types of caring response were identified, two for each type of moral situation:

1. Direct benevolent response — in which a caring person has a direct desire for others' welfare in situations not requiring adjudication.
2. Dutiful benevolent response — in which a caring person desires to fulfill a duty in situations not requiring adjudication.
3. Direct just response — in which a caring person has a direct desire that those in a conflict are treated fairly.
4. Dutiful just response — in which a caring person desires to fulfill a duty in situations which require adjudication.

Each of these will be elaborated in the next few pages.

Benevolent Response

Immanuael Kant wrote that "If . . . there is no way in which I can be of help to the sufferer and I can do nothing to alter his situation, I might as well turn coldly away."[26] Contrary to Kant, it can clearly be psychologically helpful to someone — for example, a dying person — if he or she knows that others care, even if they can do nothing. A person benefits from care not only as a result of helping actions but also from knowing that another cares. As Lawrence Blum says: "It is good to us merely that someone . . . cares about our weal and woe."[27]

> Suppose I have a flat tire by the side of the highway, my jack is broken, and there is no phone nearby. I am dependent on a passing car to stop. When, eventually, Manero stops to help me, I am greatly relieved that

my tire is changed so I can get on the road again, and I value Manero's act of beneficence for this reason. But, in addition, I would naturally value Manero's act as expressive of the human sympathy and compassion it showed in Manero's taking the trouble to stop and help me. If I had reason to believe that the act was not expressive of such sympathy and compassion — e.g., if Manero had a kind of business connected with his auto repair shop, in which he carried tire-fixing equipment around with him and offered for a fee to fix the tires of persons in my sort of situation — then I would regard, and value, the act differently. Though it would still have the substantial value to me of relieving my helpless situation and enabling me to drive my car . . . it would lack the element of human sympathy or compassion. For Manero would be doing the act purely . . . as a business proposition. The good to me of the two different acts would differ.[28]

Although Blum's example refers to emotions, it is better understood with respect to benevolent desire. What is important about this example is its making clear that it is not the act alone which distinguishes one response from another. Although the act of fixing the car is the same regardless of Manero's motivation, the response is not the same. One response includes the desire for another's welfare while the other response includes a desire for self-enhancement. If Manero's action is done to enhance his business, it is not a caring action at all; rather it is a prudent or self-interested action.

It is not possible to be directly aware of what another desires. Because action alone does not indicate the nature of a response, knowing whether another cares is partially dependent on knowing how another consistently acts in moral situations. One is also able to determine the sincerity of a response as a result of corresponding emotions but only if the "helper" has the ability to express the emotion he or she experiences.

A benevolent response consists of a benevolent desire for another's welfare as well as a corresponding caring emotion. A benevolent response also includes an action in those situations where an action is possible. It is clear that not acting when one is able to act is a morally deficient response, even though desiring another's welfare and experiencing regret or guilt for not acting are both morally significant.

Dutiful Benevolent Response

I have argued that it is not practically possible for someone specifically to desire the welfare of all sentient beings in all situations. In those situations in which a caring person does not have a specific desire for another, he or she will desire to fulfill a duty of benevolence. To desire to do one's duty is to be conscientious.

In situations in which a caring person does not directly desire another's welfare, this person acknowledges a duty of benevolence. To acknowledge a duty is to remind oneself, at the time of a moral response, of those reasons which justify responding benevolently in the particular situation. One's response is motivated by a desire to act on these reasons. Because someone is motivated by duty rather than directly by those in a predicament, emotional experience is different.

In those situations in which it is possible to respond directly to others, a dutiful benevolent response is less morally significant than a direct benevolent response. The process of reminding oneself of reasons which justify responding detracts from the morality of the response. Moreover, there may be some delay in completing the response as a result of reminding oneself what it is about this situation which is morally compelling.

> The conscientious attitude is one which involves the thought of good or of pleasure for someone else, but it is a more reflective attitude than that in which we aim directly at the production of some good or some pleasure for another, since in it the mere thought of some particular good, or of a particular pleasure for another does not immediately incite us to action, but we stop to think whether in all the circumstances the bringing of that good or pleasure is what is really incumbent on us.[29]

Contrast the response of someone who desires to help an elderly man who trips and falls with the response of someone who sees the elderly man fall and pauses to consider whether this situation is morally compelling. If the second person determines that she is morally justified in acting, her lack of spontaneity to the man's predicament allows a longer time for him to suffer. Moreover, her pause to reflect indicates that her primary concern is not with the welfare of the man but with doing what a caring person would do.

As I indicated in the last chapter, I am not suggesting that there is no moral significance in acting from duty. A caring person is not able to respond with a direct benevolent desire in all situations in which others could be helped. However, in those situations in which it is possible to respond directly and someone only recognizes a duty to be benevolent, the response *is* morally deficient. In other words, a moral response which requires reminding oneself of what is morally important is less morally significant than a response which is made directly as a result of another's predicament. A dutiful benevolent response is less morally signficant in situations in which it is possible to respond directly because this response only indirectly focusses on those in a moral situation.

There will be situations in which a caring person who initially responds from a duty of benevolence comes to desire the welfare of those in a situation as a result of being involved in the situation. For example, if I am trying to get to a concert on time and I see someone fall in the street, I may initially stop to help because, although wanting to hurry to the concert, I recognize that I have a duty to help people who are hurt. In the course of responding from duty I may recognize the suffering of this person *qua* person and desire to proceed because of this.[30]

Just Response

I argued in chapter 3 that, in situations which require adjudication of conflict, a caring person can, without contradiction, desire that people *qua* people are treated fairly and, at the same time, be impartial to the personal features of those in a conflict. Naomi Scheman claims that impartiality is all we want from those who adjudicate conflicts and it matters not if they care about us. What we want, she says,

> . . . is attentive listening (asking the right questions, taking the answers seriously), careful consideration of possible causes of action. . . . We don't expect them to have any particular feeling for us. . . . If their thoughts and emotions are elsewhere, if they don't even like us especially well, if they forget about us as soon as their work is done — fine.[31]

Responding only on the basis of feeling badly for someone will likely lead to an unfair response. On the other hand, responding without caring that those in a conflict are treated fairly is less morally significant if it is possible to care. It is morally significant if an adjudicator desires fair treatment for those in a predicament while retaining the impartiality necessary to provide relevant adjudicating reasons. Emotion experienced by an adjudicator both during a conflict and as a result of whether fair treatment is attained is also a morally significant part of this response. As with a direct benevolent response, if someone is to gain some good from another caring about his or her fair treatment, a caring person will need to express these emotions adequately.

If those in a conflict are to be treated fairly, there must be reasons which reflect how each is to be treated fairly. These adjudicating reasons are a necessary part of just responses (Karen tells the waiters why the tip money should be distributed in a certain way). In some instances, although not all, it is also essential that some action is performed. It is not enough, for example, for a school principal to provide reasons which indicate that fair treatment entails that both boys and girls benefit from physical education programs and then do nothing to ensure that both actually do benefit. Or, for example, it is not enough for someone to articulate that fair treatment entails that the Native Peoples, the working class, women, and disabled people should benefit from education and not then do something about social structures which may make this impossible. Whether a desire for fair treatment also requires denunciation of personal privilege and power is something I will address later in this chapter when discussing extraordinary caring responses.

Dutiful Just Response

For various reasons a caring person will be involved in situations as an adjudicator while not having a specific desire to treat others in the situation fairly. In these situations, if someone is caring, he or she will desire to fulfill a duty of justice. The dutiful just response includes all three types of reasons outlined earlier. Since a dutiful just response is not motivated by a direct desire for another's fair treatment, it includes acknowledging reasons which justify responding justly in a particular instance. This conscientious desire to do one's duty based on these justifying reasons, together with relevant beliefs, is the motivating reason for a response. These and the reasons provided to adjudicate a particular situation make up the dutiful just response.

Someone who acts from duty does not experience an emotion as a result of what happens to those in a conflict. The emotion which is experienced is a result of whether dutiful desire is fulfilled or thwarted. Someone who desires to act from a duty of justice experiences anger, for example, when the principle of justice is disregarded. Because emotion is not experienced as a result of a conflict being resolved for those in a conflict, a dutiful just response is less morally significant to those in the situation than a direct just response.

It is possible that someone may initially respond dutifully to those requiring fair treatment and, as a result of being involved, come to desire directly the fair treatment of those in the moral situation. For example, if I am asked to adjudicate a conflict between two students wishing to make the same class presentation, I may initially respond from duty but, as I become more involved, I may desire that the conflict be resolved amicably and fairly because it becomes important to me that the two particular students be treated fairly.

Extraordinary Caring Response

J. O. Urmson gives an example of a squad of soldiers practising the throwing of live hand grenades. A grenade slips on the ground near the squad and one of the soldiers throws himself on the grenade to protect his comrades with his own body.[32] This is a moral action, says Urmson, even though nobody could have said that the soldier ought to have thrown himself on the grenade nor could anyone have ordered him to do it. The soldier is clearly morally superior to the other soldiers, according to Urmson, although we do not blame the other soldiers for not doing the action. The soldier's action is supererogatory because it goes beyond what a person is normally thought to have a duty to do. Giving up one's job to go to Ethiopia to help the starving is another example of an action which we praise people for doing but do not blame them if they do not do.

> . . . supererogation is primarily attributed to *acts* or *actions* rather than to persons, traits of character, motives, intentions, or emotions. Secondly these acts are *optional* or *non-obligatory*, that is distinguished from those acts which fall under the heading of duty. Thirdly, they are *beyond* duty, fulfill *more* than is required, *over and above* what the agent is supposed or expected to do. This means that although they are distinguished from obligatory acts, they are not just a different moral category but stand in specific relationship . . . to obligatory action. Finally, this relationship implies that supererogatory acts have a special value; they are *morally good* and praiseworthy.[33]

Since supererogation is conceptually linked to duty and not to character, it is important to examine whether supererogation is a helpful concept when attempting to understand the scope of caring responses. I have argued that the morality of duty complements the morality of character in those situations in which someone does not directly care that those in a moral situation are treated well or fairly. To be able to act from duty is essential to a caring person in those situations in which the welfare or fair treatment of others is not desired. Even so, supererogation is not a useful concept in relation to caring responses because supererogation is conceptually tied only to duty and not to motivation. Since motivation is crucial to differentiating a caring person from, say, a self-interested person, a different concept is required to account for those responses in which people do extraordinary things for others.

Since it is possible to perform an extraordinary caring response without first recognizing a duty, supererogation does not account for extraordinary caring responses. Supererogatory action can only be performed by those who act from duty. It is not possible to account for the response of a person who goes to Ethiopia to help unless that person first recognizes a duty to help others in more proximate cases. There are people, however, who help others not from duty but because they desire to help them, and whose breadth and intensity of caring are such that this care extends much beyond proximate cases to include those as far away as Ethiopia. If someone desires to help directly those starving in Ethiopia and if the person acts on this desire, it does not make sense to say that this action is a supererogatory action since this person does not recognize a duty which he or she then goes beyond. On the other hand, if someone almost always refers to duty in moral situations and seldom directly desires the welfare of those in moral situations, it seems unlikely that in difficult moral situations, this person would go beyond the acknowledged duty to desire others' welfare.

The same point can be made about just responses. A caring person has a general desire that others are treated fairly. Because it is practically impossible directly to desire fair treatment of all others, if only because one cannot know about all conflicts, there are occasions in which a caring person acts from a desire to fulfill a duty of justice. If extraordinary just responses are restricted to those responses which go beyond duty, extraordinary just actions cannot be performed by those who respond directly to others. But there are people whose direct desire for justice for others is far reaching and who do not act from duty. Moreover, it does not make sense that, if someone regularly refers to duty and seldom directly desires others' fair treatment, in difficult situations, he or she would go beyond duty directly to desire others' fair treatment.

I have said that care implies a desire for social change so that welfare and fair treatment can be achieved. An extraordinary just action would be one that would create substantial change in one's life as one attempted to achieve social change. For example, a white, middle-class man performs an extraordinary just action when he not only works for the fair treatment of blacks, women, or the working class, but also renounces his own privileges. Such renunciation would be an extraordinary just response.

An extraordinary caring response does not go beyond duty. It does not go beyond duty because no duty has been recognized. It is a response which is performed by a caring person whose specific benevolent or just desires extend beyond that for which a person is normally blamed if an action is not performed.

Notes

1. Lawrence Blum makes this point in *Friendship, Altruism and Morality* (London: Routledge and Kegan Paul, 1980) with respect to the moral significance of moral emotions. See page 144.
2. Blum, p. 145.
3. It might be argued that there are situations which require adjudication but which do not require providing reasons at the time of the response. For example, I may have the responsibility of dividing a piece of cake for two other people. When cutting and serving the pieces of cake I do not provide reasons for the way I divided the cake. This is so only if I have divided the cake evenly. If I have not divided the cake evenly, then it is incumbent upon me to indicate the reasons why I think one person should have a larger piece of cake than another.
4. Parts of this section were presented in a paper entitled, "Education of Moral Emotions" to the Canadian Association of Foundations Education, Learned Society Meeting, Hamilton, Ontario, 3 June 1987.

5. G. Pitcher, "Emotion," in *Education and the Development of Reason*, eds. R. F. Dearden, P. H. Hirst, and R. S. Peters (London: Routledge and Kegan Paul, 1972), p. 380.
6. William James, *Principles of Psychology*, Vol. II (New York: Macmillan, 1890), pp. 449-50.
7. Magda Arnold, *The Nature of Emotion* (New York: Penguin Books, 1968), p. 46.
8. William Lyons, *Emotion* (Cambridge: Cambridge University Press, 1980), p. 155.
9. Lyons, p. 22.
10. This is R. S. Peters's example from "Motivation, Emotion and the Conceptual Schemes of Common Sense," in *Psychology and Ethical Development* (London: George Allen and Unwin Ltd., 1974).
11. José Ortega y Gasset, *The Dehumanization of Art* (Garden City, New Jersey: Doubleday and Co., Anchor Books, 1956), p. 14.
12. Ortega, p. 14.
13. Lyons, *Emotion*, p. 35.
14. Lyons, p. 50.
15. Pitcher, "Emotion," p. 373.
16. R. S. Peters, "The Education of the Emotions," in *Psychology and Ethical Development*, p. 178.
17. Jerome Shaffer, "An Assessment of Emotion," *American Philosophical Quarterly* 20 (1983): 166.
18. Lyons, *Emotion*, p. 57.
19. Lyons, p. 57.
20. Shaffer, "An Assessment of Emotion," p. 163.
21. Bernard Williams, "Morality and the Emotions," in *Problems of the Self* (Cambridge: At the University Press, 1973), p. 228.
22. I am grateful to William Hare for making this point in response to my paper "Education of Moral Emotions."
23. Shaffer, "An Assessment of Emotion," p. 165.
24. Although some domestic animals may benefit from sincere display of emotion, most animals will not. Even though most animals are unable to discern someone's motivation, a distinction can still be made between someone who responds directly to animals as beings in this world and someone who perfunctorily responds to them.
25. Shaffer rightly points out that "there are disadvantages to this arrangement. We can be misled; physiological/psychological states can be feigned or suppressed, and their presence or absence can be misinterpreted" (p. 167).
26. Immanuel Kant, *Lectures on Ethics*, translated by L. Infield (New York: Harper and Row, 1963), p. 200.
27. Lawrence Blum, *Friendship, Altruism, and Morality*, p. 221n.
28. Blum, p. 144.
29. W. D. Ross, *The Right and the Good* (Oxford: Clarendon Press, 1930), p. 163.
30. I am grateful to Elaine Nay for this point.
31. Naomi Scheman, "On Sympathy," *The Monist* 62 (1970): 322.
32. J. O. Urmson, "Saints and Heroes," in *Essays in Moral Philosophy*, ed. A. I. Melden (Seattle: University of Washington Press, 1958).
33. David Heyd, *Supererogation: Its Status in Ethical Theory* (Cambridge: Cambridge University Press, 1982), p. 1.

5

∞ Care and Gender ∞

This chapter will touch upon work on care and gender, specifically that of Carol Gilligan and Nel Noddings.[1] In so doing I want to distinguish my own account of care from theirs and to argue against dichotomization of moral theory into a feminine ethic of care and a masculine ethic of justice. At the same time, however, I want to emphasize the importance of recognizing that women and men do tend to experience their moral agency differently. Not to recognize this would be to remain ignorant of another of the many ways experiences are gendered.[2]

Carol Gilligan

In her book *In A Different Voice*, Carol Gilligan counters Lawrence Kohlberg's portrayal of a moral person as someone who is separate from others and who rationally obeys moral principles reflecting human rights. By claiming that someone has reached the highest stage of moral development when able to use universal principles of justice, Kohlberg ignores any reference to character, motivation, or emotions (what he calls "the bag of virtues"[3]). Benevolence is rejected as part of morality because, as Kohlberg says, benevolence does not resolve problems in which interests conflict.[4] "Most social situations," Kohlberg writes, "are not moral because there is no conflict between the role taking expectations of one person and another."[5]

Kohlberg's "justice perspective" has its basis in the philosophical work of Kant and Rawls as well as years of empirical work interpreted exclusively, as it turns out, from responses of boys and men. As is common in research, the experience of these boys and men was claimed by Kohlberg to be a universal experience of moral development. However, girls and women have not scored as well as boys and men on assessment of moral reasoning designed from the results of boys and men's experiences. Rather than recognize that the assessment procedure might be deficient, the maturity of women's moral judgment has been called into question.[6]

In opposition to Kohlberg, Gilligan argues that the "justice perspective" is not the only perspective on moral development and moral agency. The "care perspective" is an alternate way which, she says, reflects how girls and women develop and experience moral problems. The girls and women in Gilligan's studies describe their responses to moral situations as a "network of connection, a web of relationships, that is sustained by a process of communication."[7] The "care perspective," with its emphasis on affection, affiliation, context, and relation, is a conception of morality which, says Gilligan, "contrasts with the formal logic of fairness that informs the justice approach."[8]

Gilligan has found that girls and women tend to provide reasons to adjudicate conflicts which emphasize relationships and connectedness rather than rights and autonomy. Gilligan's results show that "men characteristically worry about people interfering with one another's rights . . . objective unfairness appears immoral to men whether or not it subjectively hurts. . . . Women worry about not helping others when they could help them, and subjectively a felt hurt appears immoral to women whether or not it is fair."[9]

Gilligan relies on the psychoanalytic work of Nancy Chodorow,[10] who explains gendered differences in interpersonal responses by the universal fact that women are responsible for early child care. Chodorow proposes that girls retain interpersonal connections while boys develop discrete identities because the primary caretaker for girls and not boys is a member of the same gender.

> One consequence of this difference is that young boys, to develop their own identity as masculine must negate their early identification with their mothers. As a result, young boys tend to see social relationships as potentially threatening to their sense of self; protection against threats to their sense of autonomy takes on a high value in their lives. Young girls on the contrary incline toward defining themselves in terms of connection to others.[11]

Whether Chodorow's explanation adequately accounts for gendered differences in moral response is the subject of debate,[12] but her explanation and Gilligan's accounts of how these differences are manifested emphasize how pervasive the sex-gender system is.

Three general comments can be made about Gilligan's work in light of my interpretation of care as moral motivation.

1. Like Kohlberg, Gilligan tends to be interested in types of reasons people give when asked about hypothetical moral situations or after certain moral situations have occurred. As Annette Baier says,

> We should not equate a person's moral stance with her intellectual version of it, nor suppose that a person necessarily knows the relative strength of her own motives and emotions. To test people's emotional and motivation growth, we would need emotion and motive experiments, and they can be tricky to design safely.[13]

Since some moral responses do not require provision of reasons of any kind (direct benevolent responses), Gilligan and Kohlberg's attempts to understand moral agency in the ways that they do make it impossible to identify moral responses which do not involve discussions about moral situations.

2. Gilligan claims that care and justice are two different and competing ethics. As important as Gilligan's demonstration of gendered differences in moral responses is, I think she is wrong to interpret these differences as an indication that there are two different and competing ethics to every moral problem[14] if by this it is suggested that morality is dichotomous. Kurt Baier says the following:

> Morality is not the preserve of an oppressed or privileged class or individual. . . . An esoteric code, a set of precepts known only to the initiated and perhaps jealously concealed from outsiders, can at best be a religion, not a morality. . . . 'Esoteric morality' is a contradiction in terms.[15]

Although Gilligan does not claim that caring is essentially a female experience of morality, she does indicate that a morality of care tends to be a common feminine experience whereas a morality of rights tends to be a masculine experience of morality. To show that women and men tend to respond in different ways in moral situations, however, is not also to show that morality is dichotomous. The logical status of a description of what is the case is not, of course, the same as the logical status of a description of what ought to be the case. Some women experience connection to others through powerlessness and dependence and some men experience autonomy through alienation and control. These experiences are not moral experiences merely because some or many women or some or many men have the experiences in moral situations. Both women's agency and men's agency in moral situations must be examined to determine if they are justifiably instances of *moral* agency.

If "subjectively a felt hurt appears immoral to women whether or not it is fair," then responding only according to "felt hurt" will not always be an appropriate moral response. This is because there are moral situa-

53

tions in which fairness is an issue. A person will be deficient as a moral agent if that person's concern with another's felt hurt prevents either recognition of a situation as one which requires adjudication or prevents one from adjudicating a conflict, even though concern for another's felt hurt is morally significant. Moral situations such as this exist, and one cannot refuse to deal with them or fail to acknowledge them as moral situations because hurt may not be resolved. Responding to these types of situations does not entail either coldly adjucating or dismissing the hurt others feel. Adjudication is an essential part of a moral response to these types of moral situations. Adjudication does not preclude feeling distressed when others are not treated fairly.

There are situations in which hurt *is* the primary moral issue. Someone who sees these situations as ones in which conflict of rights is at stake or who does not recognize these situations at all will, likewise, be deficient as a moral agent in these type of situations.

Whatever way gender differences in moral situations are interpreted, it is essential to remember that what people do and what they ought to do in moral situations is often very different. If we do not make this distinction, we eliminate the possibility of determining whether what people do is morally justifiable; we eliminate the possibility that what is done is justifiable for those outside a particular group; and consequently, we make certain moral responses inaccessible to those outside this group.

Avoiding dichotomization of morality does not mean, however, that we ignore that women and men do tend to experience their moral agency differently. We must attend to this in order to better understand the ways in which and the reasons why experiences are often gendered. It is particularly important that we develop a better understanding of women's experiences of morality. If men's experiences of morality continue to inform moral theory, we risk girls and women experiencing what Kathryn Morgan describes as "moral madness."[16]

3. When care is understood as moral motivation, it is not appropriate to say, as does Gilligan, that every moral problem can be seen from *either* a care or justice perspective.[17] I have argued that someone can both care that others are treated well and care that others are treated fairly.

Justice does not preclude connection to those in a conflict. Indeed, someone is connected to others in a conflict when directly desiring their fair treatment. Rather than see someone who separates from others as responding from a justice perspective, I would like to suggest instead that someone who separates is someone who does not directly desire others' welfare or fair treatment. (Someone who does not place *any* value on connections with others will likely not respond either directly or indirectly to others in moral situations.[18]) Responding indirectly from duty is not restricted to situations requiring fair treatment, however. Responding from duty can also occur in situations which do not require adjudication — in situations in which the welfare of others is at stake.

Gilligan, like Kohlberg, only considers moral situations in which there are conflicts to adjudicate. Because of her exclusive concern with moral conflict, she ironically limits caring situations to those requiring justice and, consequently, confines her understanding of the moral domain to those situations in which a moral agent must provide moral reasons which adjudicate a conflict. She ignores those moral situations which do not involve provision of reasons to resolve conflicts — that is, situations requiring a benevolent response.

I want to emphasize that care and justice are not appropriately contrasted since a caring person cares that others are treated well *and* that they are treated fairly. It might be argued that Gilligan uses care in the same way that I use benevolence. I don't think this is so since Gilligan concerns herself only with situations requiring adjudication and because these types of situations cannot be approached from a benevolence perspective. Benevolence is specific to those situations in which others' welfare is affected and no adjudication is required, while justice is specific to situations in which fair treatment is affected in a conflict resolution. What Gilligan does mean by care is interpersonal connection which is possible, I have shown, in both benevolent and just responses.

Rather than interpret women's tendency to connect to others as an indication that women are not concerned with justice, an argument might be made that some types of connection, at least, are an indication of a direct desire for others' welfare and fair treatment. I will elaborate this argument later in the chapter. Before I do that I want to say something about the moral status of interpersonal connection by looking at another book on care, *Caring: A Feminine Approach to Ethics and Moral Education,* by Nel Noddings. This will also allow me to highlight some distinctions between Noddings's account of care and my own.

Nel Noddings

Caring: A Feminine Approach to Ethics and Moral Education is an important book because it is the first systematic attempt in the moral education literature to acknowledge care as morally significant. Whereas, moral education has traditionally focussed on the development of an ability to understand moral reasons, moral language, and procedural principles, Noddings contends that the aim of all education "must be maintenance and enhancement of caring."[19]

Noddings is correct to claim that the focus of care is on others and not on rules, reasons, and procedural principles all of which translate human relationships into abstractions. To care for another, according to Noddings, is to be engrossed in the other, to receive the other's concerns, and to displace one's motivational energy toward the other. "Our attention," says Noddings, ". . . is on the cared-for, not on ourselves."[20]

Noddings rightly suggests that caring people function at two levels, although her account of these is not entirely correct. Noddings recognizes that even though the focus of care is on others, it is not always possible to care in the same way about all others.

> If by "I love everyone" I mean that I would not without just cause harm anyone, that is acceptable. It is not trivial, for there are those who would harm others for their own worldly gain. But it is wildly ambiguous. If that is all I mean when I say that I love my child, or my husband, or my student, then each of these has, I think, been cheated.[21]

Noddings recognizes that, in those instances in which we do not care about others, we acknowledge an obligation or duty to respond to those in a moral situation. Noddings claims, however, that what determines whether care is focussed on another or on an obligation is whether this person is a friend or a family member.

The two levels of caring response described by Noddings are what she calls natural caring and ethical caring. Natural caring, she says, has its origins in the mother-child relationship; it comes to us naturally and requires no "ethical effort." Ethical caring, on the other hand, requires an effort and comes to us as an obligation. "Indeed", she says, "the caring person . . . dreads the proximate stranger, for she cannot easily reject the claim he has on her. She would prefer that the stray cat not appear at the back door — or the stray teenager at the front."[22] Care for family and friends, according to Noddings, is willing care. Care for strangers is extended only unwillingly. I believe that it is arbitrary to suggest that care for family and friends is always spontaneous or that "care" for strangers is dreaded and in need of effort. Contrary to Noddings, we do not think of someone as caring if this person hopes to remain ignorant of strangers' misfortunes in order to avoid obligation. Care is not circumscribed by friends and family; and, in those situations in which one can respond directly, care is incompatible with obligation. Noddings's so-called ethical caring person is very much like the moral person of traditional moral philosophy whom she criticizes: one who is detached from others and who responds only after referring to reasons which show that there is an obligation to do so. I have argued, on the other hand, that a caring person is someone who responds directly to those in moral situations, when it is possible to do so, and that it is not only possible to do this when moral situations involve friends and family.

Noddings argues that there must be reciprocity if care is to be care. By this she means that the "cared-for" must perceive the "one-caring" as caring if care is to occur. The "one-caring" does not *really* care, she claims, if the person "cared-for" does not care about the "one-caring": "X does not feel that I care. Therefore, sadly, I must admit that, while I feel that I care, X does not perceive that I care, and hence, the relationship cannot be characterized as one of caring."[23] This is clearly a stipulation. I do not cease to care that my friend not suffer in the hospital when it becomes apparent that she isn't aware that I care. My care that she becomes well may be morally significant to her when she knows that I care but my care does not cease if my friend is, for example, in a coma and isn't aware of me or my benevolent desire. According to Noddings, the relationship between reciprocity and care entails some sort of response by the particular "cared-for" either directly or indirectly through "personal delight or in happy growth before her eyes."[24] My position, on the other hand, is that there need not be reciprocity in each encounter in order for care to take place, although I do think that care must be shared by people in a community. Care must be shared by those in a community because it is not possible for only a few people to affect circumstances so that all are treated well and fairly and because, without the sharing of care, certain individuals, most often women, will live lives of self-sacrifice. Reciprocity is not required in each caring encounter but there is a need for "reciprocity in the actions, expectations, and claims of the group."[25]

In an earlier work, Noddings claims that "caring reduces the necessity for justice"[26] because, as I understand her, fewer conflicts will occur between people if they are cared for. Still, we must account for those situations in which it is necessary to adjudicate conflicts fairly when they do occur between others. A caring person cares that the individuals in these situations are treated fairly. Contrary to Noddings, justice is not appropriately contrasted to care, and benevolence is not appropriately made synonymous with care, as I have said, since one can care that others are treated justly and care that others are helped.

Noddings refers to the "one-caring" as female and the "cared-for" as male. She says she does this to "maintain balance and avoid confusion." The depiction of women as "ones-caring" fairly accurately reflects, however, Carol Gilligan's research which shows that women do tend to be the "ones-caring." Reference to women as the "one's caring" and men as those "cared-for" has interesting implications if reciprocity, as understood by Noddings, is a necessary condition of caring. If it is the case that boys and men tend not to care and, if they are also usually the "cared-for," then, with reciprocity being essential in individual relationships, care would be an uncommon phenomenon at least between women and men and between men.

Although Gilligan and Noddings both describe care as representative of experiences of moral agency which girls and women tend to have, Noddings restricts care to situations in which others' welfare is at stake while Gilligan restricts care to those moral situations which require fair adjudication of moral conflicts. What Gilligan and Noddings have in common is the moral significance they place on human relations and connections.

In light of what I have said about the necessity of shared caring in a community in order that some do not live lives of self-sacrifice, it is legitimate to question whether interpersonal connections may, at times, be morally problematic. Connection, affiliation, and relation, often thought to be ethical virtues for women, are often also associated with their oppression. Noddings, perhaps inadvertently, captures a source of the problem by referring to the "one-caring" as feminine and the "cared-for" as masculine. Desire for others' welfare and fair treatment is one way we can connect to others, but connection to others is also necessary for relationships in which someone is, for example, submissive, powerless, dependent, and guileful.[27] Certain kinds of connections are not caring connections at all. Some very profound connections to another can occur without either person in a relationship desiring the other's welfare or fair treatment. Connection to others is not always morally significant. Connection is morally significant when it is indicative of motivation to help others and treat them fairly.

Just as women are not necessarily moral because they tend to connect with others, men are not necessarily moral by virtue of a tendency to separate from others. Exclusion, self-centredness, and uncommunicativeness are all forms that autonomy can take. These would clearly inhibit someone from responding to another in a moral situation. Autonomy is an important attribute insofar as it enables someone to adjudicate moral conflicts impartially. Autonomy is also important in order to avoid those submissive, powerless, dependent relationships which involve self-sacrifice and often loss of self-identity. If autonomy is understood as the opposite of connection, when by connection is meant care, then autonomy is inimical to care. But, if autonomy is understood as an attribute that a caring person must have in order to avoid being one of only a few caring people in a community and in order to adjudicate certain types of moral situations impartially, autonomy is an essential attribute of a caring person.

In the next chapter I will have something more to say about attributes which in some situations aid a caring person but which can equally aid an immoral person. Here, however, I want to emphasize that neither connection nor autonomy are moral attributes in every moral situation. Consequently, any attempt to show that women are more moral because of a tendency to connect or that men are more moral because of a tendency to be autonomous must show, on independent grounds, what it is about each of these that is moral.

Gender and Duty

Gilligan thinks that there are two perspectives to every moral problem: the care perspective and the justice perspective. I believe that if consideration is given to moral situations which do not require adjudication as well as those which do, and if consideration is given to moral agency at the time of a moral response rather than in reflection about it, the two perspectives that Gilligan's results seem to show can be described instead as a "direct care perspective" and a "duty perspective." Given my account of the differences between a direct response to others and a dutiful response to others, it may be possible to see those who are concerned with interpersonal connections as people who directly respond to others both in moral situations in which others' welfare is at stake and in situations in which fair treatment is at stake. Those who are concerned with autonomy and rights may, on the other hand, be seen as people who desire to fulfill a duty both in situations in which others' fair treatment is affected and in situations in which others' welfare is affected. Women may tend to fit the first description and men may tend to fit the second description. It is important to note, however, that both women and men are faced with moral situations in which it is not possible directly to desire others' welfare or fair treatment and, therefore, both women and men must be able to respond to duty. Clearly, also, on some occasions, both women and men do respond directly to others in moral situations.[28]

Seeing the two perspectives as a direct care perspective and a duty perspective rather than a care perspective and a justice perspective may also help in understanding what appears to be a difference in emotional response between women and men in moral situations. If women do tend to be more emotional in moral situations than men, it might be because women tend directly to desire others' welfare and fair treatment while men tend to desire to fulfill duties. As was discussed in chapter 4, one has an emotional experience concomitantly when one desires that someone is treated well or fairly. An emotional experience occurs both during the moral situation and when it is determined whether one's benevolent or just desire is fulfilled or thwarted. A desire that a duty be done, on the other hand, has a concomitant emotion usually only when it is determined whether one's desire that a duty be fulfilled is fulfilled or not.

Experience of an emotion does not mean, however, that someone will express the emotions experienced. Expression of emotion by women may be explained by the fact that emotional display is more socially acceptable by women than by men. Both insufficient display and superfluous display of emotion may detract from the potential moral significance to a recipient of a moral response. Insufficient display of emotion may not convey enough information to a recipient of a moral response. Superfluous display of emotion may interfere with other essential parts of a moral response, for example, adjudication or providing life-saving skills. The commonly held belief that women tend not to control the expression of their emotions while men do is, of course, problematic. Men often express emotions through aggressive or violent behavior while women tend to express their emotions by crying.[29]

Because morality is often dichotomized according to gender, and rationality is considered to be a component of masculine morality while emotionality is considered to be a component of feminine morality, it is important to emphasize again that someone is not only rational or only emotional in response to moral situations. If someone's motivating reason for a response is another's welfare or fair treatment, she or he will necessarily experience an emotion both during a particular moral situation and in response to its outcome.

A reliance on reasons in a moral response is not sufficient to indicate that someone approaches a moral situation from a justice perspective. Approaching a moral situation from a duty perspective also requires acknowledging reasons. Situations requiring fair treatment involve providing adjudicating reasons while situations in which someone responds from duty involve acknowledging justifying reasons. If men's responses to moral situations tend to reflect justifying reasons, this may be an indication that men may respond more often to duty than directly to those in a moral situation. If men tend to provide adjudicating reasons in their responses at the time of a moral response and women tend not to provide reasons at all at the time of a moral response, this may be an indication that women tend to respond more often to situations in which others' welfare is at stake (a direct response to this situation does not require provision of reasons at the time of the response), and it may be an indication that men tend to respond more often to situations in which others' fair treatment is at stake (a direct response to this situation requires provision of adjudicating reasons). I do not believe that Gilligan's results show this, however, since she is concerned only with situations in which there is a conflict and consequently both women and men in her examples are required to provide reasons to adjudicate these conflicts.

If men do tend to respond from a justice perspective while women tend to respond from a care or benevolence perspective, it does not then follow that there is a justice and care perspective to every moral situation. Rather, it is an indication that social expectations and experiences of women and men prepare them differently for two fundamentally different moral tasks.

If there are tendencies for women to respond to situations requiring benevolence and for men to respond to situations requiring justice, these tendencies may mirror a private-public split in which situations requiring benevolence rather than justice are more prevalent in the private sphere, while situations requiring justice rather than benevolence are more prevalent in the public sphere. However, even if this is the case, moral situations do not neatly divide up in this way. People do not cease to become injured, or to be troubled, or to become distraught when they undertake public functions. A benevolent response is as appropriate in public as it is in private when welfare is at stake. So too, conflicts do not only occur in public institutions and adjudication is not only the purview of those who fill institutional roles. Conflicts requiring fair adjudication also occur between friends and family members and this adjudication is often performed by other friends and family members.

It is significant that the adjudicating reasons women tend to provide for resolution of conflicts are ones which focus on the connection and interpersonal relations of people. This, I have said, may reflect direct desire for fair treatment of those in conflicts. Autonomy and a focus on rights, evident in many men's responses, may indicate what men find relevant when adjudicating conflicts, or the reasons men tend to provide may reflect a reliance on duty. All of this is, of course, highly speculative on my part, but I think that such speculation points to the possibility of interpreting Gilligan's empirical evidence in alternative ways.

Speculation about the interpretation of different experiences of moral agency according to gender in this chapter underlines the importance of recognizing the complexity of a concept like care. It is important to understand, for example, that not just any interpersonal connection is a caring connection; that autonomy is sometimes important to a caring person; that both reason and emotion play a role in a caring response; that a caring person cares as much about treating others fairly as helping them; that a caring person sometimes needs to act from duty; and that none of these ought to be more important to one gender than to another.

Notes

1. Carol Gilligan, *In A Different Voice: Psychological Theory and Women's Development* (Cambridge: Harvard University Press, 1982). Nel Noddings, *Caring: A Feminine Approach to Ethics and Moral Education* (Berkeley: University of California Press, 1984).
2. Sex and gender are often used in order to distinguish biological sex differences of females and males from the socially constructed expectations of biological females and males to conform to feminine and masculine behaviors. The social

organization of biological females and males produces feminine gendered behavior in girls and women and masculine gendered behavior in boys and men.

The relationship of sex and gender is more complex than these categories suggest, however, as the following passage indicates. The passage is from Alison Jaggar's "Human Biology in Feminist Theory: Sexual Equality Reconsidered," in *Beyond Domination: New Perspectives on Women and Philosophy,* ed. Carol C. Gould (Totowa, New Jersey: Rowman and Allanheld, 1984), pp. 36-37:

> "The effects of each of these factors cannot be isolated because each affects and changes the others. . . . human biology, like the physical environment, is not just a pre-social given, remaining constant throughout the changes in human social life. Instead, it is a result as well as a cause of our system of social organization. This is as true of sex differences as of other aspects of human biology. . . . In general women have been prevented from developing their capacities for physical speed and strength, and the effects of this prohibition can be seen simply by looking at women's bodies, particularly their upper bodies. The rate at which women's athletic records are being broken and the speed with which women's bodies have changed even over the past decade shows that in the past, social norms have limited the way in which women fulfilled their genetic potential, so that we have no idea of the extent of that potential."

3. Lawrence Kohlberg, "Education of Justice: A Modern Statement of the Platonic View," in *Moral Education: Five Lectures,* eds. N. F. Sizer and T. R. Sizer (Cambridge: Harvard University Press, 1970), p. 63.
4. Lawrence Kohlberg, "From Is to Ought," in *Cognitive Development and Epistemology,* ed. Theodore Mischel (New York: Academic Press, 1971), p. 220.
5. Kohlberg, p. 192.
6. Diane T. Meyers and Eva Feder Kittay, "Introduction" in *Women and Moral Theory* (Totowa, N.J.: Rowman and Littlefield, 1987), p. 6. For discussions on the link of moral rationality with masculinity see, for example, Lawrence Blum, "Kant's and Hegel's Moral Rationalism: A Feminist Perspective," *Canadian Journal of Philosophy* 12 (1982): 287-300, and Genevieve Lloyd, *The Man of Reason: Male and Female in Western Philosophy* (London: Methuen, 1984).
7. Gilligan, *In A Different Voice,* p. 33.
8. Gilligan, p. 73.
9. Sandra Harding, "Is Gender a Variable in Conceptions of Rationality: A Survey of Issues," *Dialectica* 36 (1982): 237-38.
10. Nancy Chodorow, *The Reproduction of Mothering: Psychoanalysis and the Sociology of Gender* (Berkeley: University of California Press, 1978).
11. Linda Nicholson, "Women, Morality and History," *Social Research* 50 (1983): 518.
12. Chodorow argues that the reproduction of mothering which results in gendered girls and boys will continue until men assume an active role in child rearing. Presumably, then, both girls and boys would develop their identifies by connecting to the like parent and separating from the unlike parent. This solution begs certain important questions, however. First, it assumes that children are only raised in two-parent, heterosexual arrangements. Second, it does

not take into account that it is gendered males who will be parenting. It has been argued that the common characteristic of masculinity is its differentiation or separation from what is feminine. (See Genevieve Lloyd, *The Man of Reason: Male and Female in Western Philosophy*, and Jean Grimshaw, *Philosophy and Feminist Thinking* (Minneapolis: University of Minnesota Press, 1986)). If this is correct, it is problematic whether boys connecting with fathers will alleviate the separation from what is feminine. Moreover, as Maureen Ford has commented to me, "mothering" may become another enterprise that men appropriate. In another way, however, Chodorow does acknowledge that it is gendered people who will be child rearing. Otherwise, connection and separation would not occur along gender lines. But, as I have said above, connection and separation along gender lines will not undermine an oppressive sex-gender system.

13. Annette Baier, "Hume, the Women's Moral Theorist," in *Women and Moral Theory*, p. 48. This point is supported by the following comment by Owen Flanagan and Kathryn Jackson in a footnote to "Justice, Care and Gender: The Kohlberg-Gilligan Debate Revised," *Ethics* 97 (1987): 628n:

> The relationship between first-person speech acts and the underlying psychology is a widely discussed issue in contemporary philosophy of mind and cognitive psychology, and there is a reason to think that our deficiencies in giving accurate self-assessments run very deep. Confabulation is an especially salient worry when the speech acts are being offered in response to issues which connect so obviously as do moral problems with issues of self-worth and with how one is perceived by others. Gilligan and Kohlberg are strangely silent on these matters.

14. See, for example, Carol Gilligan, "Moral Orientation and Moral Development," in *Women and Moral Theory*.

15. Kurt Baier, *The Moral Point of View* (New York: Random House, 1965), p. 101.

16. Kathryn Pauly Morgan, "Women and Moral Madness," a paper presented to the Canadian Society of Women in Philosophy, Montreal, 1984.

17. Gilligan, "Moral Orientation and Moral Development," p. 20.

18. As long as someone lives in a community of some kind, one cannot deny that he or she is connected to others. One may see oneself as separate from others, but all social relations require connection of some kind.

19. Noddings, *Caring: A Feminine Approach to Ethics and Moral Education*, p. 172.

20. Noddings, *Caring: A Feminine Approach to Ethics and Moral Education*, p. 87. Unfortunately, Noddings also says that the answer to the question, " 'Why should I behave morally?' [is] 'because I am or want to be a moral person' " (p. 50). It is contradictory to say that one cares about someone else if "motivational energy" is actually directed at oneself in an attempt to confirm oneself as a "moral" being.

21. Noddings, p. 112.

22. Noddings, p. 47.

23. Noddings, p. 68.

24. Noddings, p. 74.

25. Seyla Benhabib, "The Generalized and the Concrete Other," in *Women and Moral Theory*, p. 175n.

26. Nel Noddings, "Caring," *Journal of Curriculum Theorizing* (1981): 147.

27. See Kathryn Pauly Morgan, "Romantic Love, Altruism, and Self-Respect," in *Women and Men: Interdisciplinary Readings on Gender,* ed. Greta Hofmann Nemiroff (Toronto: Fitzhenry and Whiteside, 1987).

28. In an article entitled "The Feminization of Love," *Signs* 11 (1986), 692-709, Francesca Cancian argues that love has two components: a nurturing component and an instrumental component. Women tend to do well in the nurturing component while men tend to do well in the instrumental or practical component. It might be argued, then, that both women and men connect with others, although they demonstrate connection in different ways. However, it can still be asked why women tend to nurture while men do not.

   In the same vein, Michael Stocker writes in "Duty and Friendship: Toward a Synthesis of Gilligan's Contrastive Moral Concepts," in *Women and Moral Theory:*
   > One person can see the world in terms of family or interpersonal responsibilities, another can see the world in terms of business or financial responsibilities. So, it might well seem that the categories of right and responsibilities do not, as such, help us make much progress. (p. 57)

   Here too, the question is why some people see interpersonal responsibilities as more important than business or financial responsibilities.

29. Although it is ironical that tears are an indication of an inability to control emotions while the display of at least some kinds of violence is not, this is another example of how what is seen to be feminine is devalued by the hierarchical sex-gender system.

6

 Other Factors Important to a Caring Response

In order for a response to be a caring response the following components are necessary: (1) There must be a moral situation to which someone can respond (a situation in which welfare or fair treatment is at stake); (2) The moral situation must be appraised or seen as a moral situation; (3) The person must be morally motivated. (He or she must have beliefs about what counts as a moral situation and he or she must desire that either welfare or fairness be enhanced depending on the situation.); (4) If the person is in a position to help or adjudicate, certain practical and/or social skills will be necessary; (5) An action to help or to adjudicate must occur if one is in a position to help or adjudicate; (6) The person responding experiences a caring emotion.

In this chapter I shall briefly say something more about the belief part of moral motivation, about appraisals, about the relationship of reasoning abilities to a caring response, and I shall show that practical and social skills are necessary to a caring response.

There are a number of other factors which, although not necessary components of a caring response, can affect whether a caring response will occur. In the previous chapter I discussed the effects that gender may have on a caring response. The factors I will discuss here are conflicting motivation, excessive or inadequate emotional display, proximity, and circumstance. For discussion purposes I present these components and factors in the order which follows.

Conflicting Motivation

There are occasions when a caring person desires something which either conflicts with a general desire that others are treated well and fairly or with a specific desire that a particular individual is treated well or fairly. If this conflicting desire is stronger than a desire to help or adjudicate fairly, the conflicting desire will override. When conflicting desires override caring desires, it is because occasionally (not permanently) a caring person has a self-interested desire, the intensity of which is greater in that particular situation than the benevolent or just desire.

Someone may, on one occasion, be self-interested and, on another occasion, desire another's welfare or fair treatment. If desire for others' welfare or fair treatment occurs only occasionally, this person is not a caring person. In other words, unless one fairly permanently desires that others are treated well and fairly, a person is not benevolent and just. An occasional desire for more for oneself is not, however, an indication that someone has the character trait of greed. But, if caring desires are often overridden, it is clear that this person is not, in fact, a caring person.

If a desire for more for oneself becomes fairly permanent it will be in opposition to the character traits of benevolence and justice. Someone will not *be* both benevolent and just and *be* avaricious.[1] Although someone may experience a number of desires which are conflicting from time to time, desires which conflict with each other cannot be permanent features of a person. If someone *is* avaricious, this person is not likely to complete a caring response except in those isolated and unexpected instances in which he or she does desire the welfare or fair treatment of someone more than he or she desires self-aggrandizement.

There are other moral character traits besides benevolence and justice, but they are only exercised as moral character traits in relation to benevolence and justice.[2] For the most part a caring person must be honest and faithful in order to treat others well and fairly. *Prima facie*, if I tell you an untruth or break my promise to you, I adversely affect you because, everything else being equal, promising that you can count on me and not following through is likely to diminish either your welfare or fair treatment.

There are other fairly permanent desires which are morally neutral. Morally neutral character traits such as courage, industry, prudence, fortitude, patience, and temperance may be of assistance to a caring person in certain moral situations. Courage, for example, is an important trait to have in those situations in which another's welfare is adversely affected and in which helping would involve personal risk. I may desire the welfare of someone who is hanging from a precipice but not do anything to help because I desire not to be hurt. If, however, I am courageous, my desire not to be hurt can be overridden and I am able to attempt to help.

Morally neutral character traits can also be useful to an immoral person, however.

> If, for instance, the dominant object of my life is to maintain, by fair means or foul, my personal power and ascendancy over some group ... I may well display, and need to display, exceptional industry in maintaining and defending my system of despotism, great courage in resisting the pressures and machinations of my opponents and enemies. . . . Thus, while the dispositions here in question are undoubted virtues, they are virtues . . . which a very bad man might have; and while probably such qualities are admirable even in a bad man, he is not . . . *morally* the better for his possession of those admirable qualities.[3]

> Courage will aid the thug, determination the pirate, patience the cracksman, gentleness the jewel thief and so on. To possess temperance or prudence is not necessarily a matter of moral praise, for these attributes can make a bad man more effective in the same way as they fortify the good man in what he attempts.[4]

Although fairly permanent neutral desires do not conflict with caring desires, when they are character traits of an immoral person, they allow him or her to be more effective as an immoral person.

Beliefs

In order to desire something, one must have some beliefs about it. If one's beliefs are inaccurate, then one's understanding of a situation changes and consequently one's motivation is affected. Having beliefs entail understanding certain concepts which, in turn, affect whether one will recognize that a situation is of a particular kind. If, for example, a child is struck by a car and someone does not have a belief that a car striking a person can be harmful and/or does not understand the concept of harm, this person will not be motivated to respond to the child who is injured. In this instance, the occurrence of a moral response depends on knowing what it is to be harmed as well as possessing some rudimentary facts about what is likely to contribute to harm. Understanding facts and concepts relevant to a moral situation does not require that one is able to give a full articulation of the facts or an explication of the necessary and sufficient conditions of the concepts involved in a belief. It is necessary, however, to have some understanding of interpersonal relationships and social institutions. As R. S. Peters says, "A child, strictly speaking, cannot be guilty of theft, who has not developed the concept of himself as distinct from others, of property, of the granting of permission, etc."[5] Someone must understand the nature of conflict, the concepts of harm and help, certain concepts entailed by social institutions, concepts associated with facts of each particular situation, and how these relate to the essential concepts of help and harm if a caring response is to be possible.

Appraisals

If someone fails to respond to a moral situation, it might be because this person does not care even though recognizing that others' welfare or fair treatment is affected. Some, however, may not respond because they do not recognize that there is a difficulty. As Stuart Hampshire writes, "moral failure is often . . . the result of . . . the narrow range of a person's perception and discrimination."[6]

A caring person is more likely to see a moral situation than someone who is not caring.

> . . . the man of sympathy and the unsympathetic (indifferent) man of duty are faced with the same or equivalent situations — persons who are in distress whom it is in each of their power to help. . . . [T]he indifferent [man] of duty is much less likely than the man of sympathy to apprehend the other person in the first place.[7]

We would be reluctant to say that someone is caring if a response occurs only when a situation is pointed out to this person. A caring person is able to see moral situations and this is part of what it is to be a caring person.

One must have beliefs about what makes a certain situation a moral situation, but one must also be able to recognize when a situation is a moral situation. Just as my beliefs about bank machines and bank cards and my desire to have money do not lead to a response if I do not see this as a situation in which it is appropriate to put my bank card in a bank machine, so I will not offer to help when I see someone looking at room numbers unless I see the situation as one in which someone is lost.

Caring people are not alone in recognizing situations in which others' welfare or fair treatment is affected. A sadist also has this ability, although the description of how the situation is seen is different for a sadistic person. A situation in which someone is hanging from a precipice is seen by a caring person as one in which another suffers *and* as an occasion for assistance, while a sadist sees the situation as one in which another suffers *and* as an occasion to take pleasure in the suffering.

An ability to recognize a moral situation is affected by an ability to imagine what it is like for others when they are in moral situations. Others can be imagined either subjectively or objectively. Anything which can have experience can be subjectively imagined; "being a king, a beggar, a cripple, a child, or a cat. . . . What is impossible is to imagine being a thing with no experience; a stone or a coffee-pot."[8] Although I cannot imagine what it would be like to be a stone or a coffee pot, I can objectively imagine what a stone or a coffee pot looks like or feels like. Objective imagination is restricted to the representation of objects which can be sensed. The lives of other people can be both subjectively and objectively imagined. I can, for example, objectively imagine what it would be like to see and hear those suffering in Ethiopia and I can subjectively imagine being an Ethiopian in these conditions. Objective imagination is essential if I am going to try to understand situations others experience. If I am to identify with another's situation I must, however, be able to imagine subjectively what this person's world is like. There is a difficulty with this. If I attempt to imagine what it would be like for you to be you, it is not possible for me to know how *I* would find the experience, if I were you.[9] It is impossible for someone to "sense from 'inside' what life is like" for another because one "remains intractably oneself "[10] with one's own perspective.

It is not necessary, however, to alter one's ontological perspective or identify with each characteristic of someone whose welfare or fair treatment is affected. Because caring people are sentient beings, it is possible to imagine other sentient beings encountering situations which affect their welfare or fair treatment. I do not need to imagine what it is like for a member of another species to be what it is, nor do I need to imagine what it would be like for *me* to be a member of another species in order to be able to identify with the suffering of another species. It is not necessary to imagine what it is like for a starving Ethiopian to be the actual person she is. Since, as a sentient being, I am able to imagine what it is like for another sentient being to starve, I am able to imagine what it would be like for her to starve.

Subjective imagination is limiting when it comes to imagining what it is like for a particular person to flourish if one does not know what counts as flourishing for that individual. Subjectively imagining what might generally contribute to the flourishing of sentient beings is of limited usefulness in particular situations because of the vast differences among people and species. As I said earlier, desiring that others flourish is likely restricted to those friends and family members about whom one knows what would count as flourishing.

Subjective imagination is closely associated with the ability to see a situation according to a particular description, but to see a situation in a particular way it is also necessary for someone to be able to imagine subjectively what it would be like to be in that situation. For example, one's subjective imagination of what it is like to be lost can be of assistance in seeing a situation as one in which someone is lost. When one sees a situation as one in which someone is lost, subjective imagination of what it is like for that particular person (child, visitor, adult) is important if one is going to respond to that person *qua* person.

Reasoning Abilities

It is assumed by many writers in moral education that moral reasoning can be reduced to an ability to differentiate moral reasons from other kinds of reasons, particularly self-interested reasons.[11] Some limit understanding of moral reasoning even more to an ability to proceed logically through a syllogism which has at least one ethical premise. For example, it is claimed in materials from the Association of Values Education and Research (A.V.E.R.) that, once someone has determined relevant facts and a value standard, the logical syllogism allows an individual to determine whether a value judgment follows logically from these facts and standards.[12] It is clear, however, that an ability to proceed logically through a syllogism is not the same as an ability to determine which facts are relevant, nor does such a skill help determine what counts as an ethical premise.

The inappropriateness of reducing either morality or moral reasoning to an ability to understand a syllogism is evident from the following example provided by Alfred Haefner, who claims that by following through a syllogism one's obligations will become clear.

> *Major premise (tripartite):* I believe that (B) praiseworthy motorists, (A) when they kill an animal on the highway, (C) are expected to stop and remove the carcass from the thoroughfare.
> *Minor premise A:* I find that I have just killed a squirrel on the highway.
> *Minor premise B:* I want to be known as a praiseworthy motorist.
> *Conclusion:* Therefore, I ought to stop and remove the dead squirrel from the road.[13]

By logically proceeding through this syllogism, one concludes that one ought to remove the dead animal from the road. What Haefner fails to see, however, is that not only does an ability to work through this syllogism not motivate anyone to act, the reasons provided for removing the animal are not moral reasons. The animal is removed in order to ensure that one can be known as a praiseworthy motorist rather than to prevent discomfort and perhaps anguish to others who will come across the animal on the road.

In chapter 4 I identified three types of moral reasoning abilities: an ability to respond to moral motivating reasons; an ability to provide moral adjudicating reasons; and an ability to acknowledge moral justifying reasons. Being deficient in one or more of these reasoning abilities will affect a caring response. Without an ability to provide adjudicating reasons, someone will not be able to function in situations in which fair treatment is essential. Without an ability to recognize justifying reasons, someone will not be able to remind oneself of what is compelling about care. And, without an ability to respond to moral motivating reasons, someone will not be a caring person at all.

In order to respond to someone who falls in the street, for example, one must be able to understand the concepts of harm and help and be able to see the situation as one in which someone is harmed. To have certain beliefs, which are, in turn, composed of certain concepts, to appraise a situation as a moral situation, and to be able to respond to these beliefs and appraisals all make up the ability to respond to motivating reasons. None of this needs to be articulated. One's understanding of moral motivating reasons is reflected in the response to the person who has fallen.

In order to respond fully to a situation requiring adjudication, a person must be able to specify how those in a particular circumstance are to receive fair treatment. This involves being able to sort out what is relevant from what is not while being sensitive to features such as race, class, gender, and disability which may bias a situation prior to an adjudication being made.

An ability to act when one has acknowledged reasons which justify responding in a particular situation is an ability which caring people require in those situations in which they do not directly desire others' welfare or fair treatment. If someone is not caring, an ability to acknowledge reasons why a situation is a moral situation is merely an intellectual skill. It is not a moral intellectual skill unless one is motivated to act on these reasons.

Emotions

I have said that caring emotions are a necessary and morally significant result of caring desires and evaluated beliefs. Emotional experience can interfere with a caring response if beliefs or evaluation of these beliefs are unreasonable or if display of emotion is either non-existent or excessive. While an emotion experienced as a result of an evaluation of another's predicament is morally significant, if an emotional experience is extreme, it may incapacitate someone from helping or adjudicating. An adjudicator may be able to adjudicate but be so overwhelmed by the plight of those in a conflict that he or she adjudicates unfairly or is unable to adjudicate at all. Similarly, someone may have an ability to provide first aid to an accident victim but be so overwhelmed with emotion that the skills are not used. In these situations, what is required is an ability to shift one's attention away from oneself to those in the predicament.

An abundant *display* of emotion may also interfere with a response. An emotionally demonstrative person may, for example, draw attention away from those in moral predicaments. On the other hand, little or no display of emotion detracts from a moral response since sincere display of emotion is what indicates motivation of someone who responds.

The moral significance of an emotional display is somewhat circumscribed by situational and cultural factors.[14] Crying, exhorting, and gesturing, which are manifestations of anger in certain cultures, for example, may be morally significant to a recipient of a moral response. But it is possible that such a display may compound this person's distress at what is seen to be an overdisplay of emotion. In another culture, however, if someone does not display emotion in this way, his or her sincerity may be doubted. To be able to display moral emotion sincerely is largely a matter of whether someone is a caring person. A caring person is not likely to feign distress at another's misfortune in order to be ingratiated with that person. A caring person is also less likely to effuse "stupid sentimentality,"[15] although, as I have said, this too may be dependent on understanding a culture's expectations. One may not always be able to display significantly an emotion commensurate to cultural expectations and, at the same time, sincerely display this emotion.

Skills and Know-how

It is conceivable that a person who recognizes a moral situation and who has no conflicting desires may still not act even when an action is possible because this person is without some relevant know-how or skill. Someone who desires to help another who is choking, drowning, cut, burned, or frost bitten but who knows nothing about life saving or first aid will not be able to help. Although the motivation to help is morally significant, if given the choice, the individual in the predicament would likely prefer the response of someone who expects a reward but who knows first aid.

Skills and know-how cannot be taken for granted once a caring person understands what it is to live in a society and how things can go wrong for others. It is inconsistent to say that I care that others not suffer from injuries but I don't care to know how to alleviate injuries when they do happen. Similarly, it is inconsistent to say that I care that others not suffer emotionally but I don't care to know how to approach people to comfort them.

If someone desires to assist others who are lost, lonely, confused, embarrassed, bereaved, disappointed, discouraged, unhappy, and so on, there is a responsibility to acquire social skills to communicate concern. If I desire to encourage someone who is standing uncomfortably apart from a group and I do nothing because I do not know how to approach this person, my caring response is deficient even though I desire to help.

Not only can one respond deficiently in situations because one is socially unskilled, one can overdo emotional expression ("stupid sentimentality," for example, may be the result of improper evaluation or insincerity but it may also be the result of inadequate social skills) or helping behaviors and as a result confound or confuse a situation.

> . . . if everyone embroils himself persistently, however well-meaningly, in other people's concerns rather than his own, a considerable measure of chaos and cross-purpose is likely to ensue.[16]

It is neither necessary nor helpful for everyone to go to Ethiopia. Overzealous "helping" may also interfere with another's agency. For example, if a parent regularly retrieves her teenager's forgotten books and lost keys and regularly reminds the teenager of appointments, the teenager may soon come to rely on the parent to do this and not, then, assume responsibility for her belongings or commitments. In some cases it is more appropriate to let someone face the consequences of his or her lack of responsibility and organization. The parent's desire for the teenager's welfare is better served if she is able to imagine both the teenager's long-term and short-term welfare.

Proximity

Physical proximity to others can make it easier to respond to others because we are able to see them as particular individuals rather than as members of humanity, persons, or sentient beings. It is impossible to respond to someone whose existence is not known; it is easier to be aware of those who are proximate than those who are distant. Proximity is a relative concept, however. There are those who care about individuals who live in remote parts of the world and there are those who need to be in very close contact with others in order even to be aware of them let alone respond to them. Proximity does allow the opportunity to identify with someone's life by virtue of seeing it close up, but being physically close does not guarantee that one will respond. Moreover, moral responses do not only occur in proximate cases. It is arbitrary to circumscribe morality within proximate encounters.

Proximity to another in a family makes it possible to be aware of another's problems as well as how this person might flourish. It is far more likely that benevolent desires directed at a family member will include a desire that this person flourish as well as a desire that he or she not suffer. Benevolent desires for strangers are limited to desires that they not suffer because, without knowledge, it is not possible to desire, in more than a general way, that a stranger flourishes. With this knowledge someone is no longer a stranger. This difference creates a barrier which separates us from strangers. Strangers are often seen as objects among other objects. Breaking down barriers between oneself and a stranger is more easily done if we are in a state of what Gabriel Marcel called *disponibilité* — a state of availability or receptiveness. If I am not available to a stranger, there will not be an opportunity for an opening to appear in the barrier which separates us. Being available means that acts of communion are possible with strangers even if, to use Buber's example, they are as fleeting as the glance between two people in an air raid shelter or between two people in a concert hall.[17] Those who are physically close will be as distant as those who are physically remote if we do not make ourselves available to them.

Circumstance

Circumstance often dictates whether someone is able to respond to a moral situation. Sometimes circumstance can be controlled and other times it cannot. Paradoxically, even when circumstance is not under the control of someone, how that person responds may still reflect morally on this person. Someone may be motivated to help another, evaluate a situation as one in which another requires help, and have requisite practical and social skills to act yet not act because of social circumstances beyond his or her control. The same action by different people in the same moral circumstance can result in a different response even when motivation is the same. This is because particular moral situations often affect people differently according to their class, race, or gender as the following episode illustrates:

> At Nevins Street, Brooklyn, we saw her preparing to get off at the next station — Atlantic Avenue — which happened to be the place where I too had to get off. Just as it was a problem for her to get on, it was going to be a problem for her to get off the subway with two small children to be taken care of, a baby on her right arm, and a medium sized valise in her left hand. . . .
> I could perceive the steep, long concrete stairs going down to the Long Island Railroad or into the street. Should I offer my help as the American white man did at the subway door placing the two children outside the subway car? Should I take care of the girl and the boy, take them by their hands until they reached the end of the steep long concrete stairs of the Atlantic Avenue Station? . . .
> But how could I, a Negro and a Puerto Rican, approach this white

lady who very likely might have preconceived prejudices against Negroes and everybody with foreign accents, in a deserted subway late at night? . . .

Here was I, way past midnight, face to face with a situation that could very well explode into an outburst of prejudices and chauvinistic conditioning of the "divide and rule" policy of present day society. . . .

I passed on by her as if I saw nothing. As if I was insensitive to her need. . . . I just moved on half running by the long subway platform leaving the children and valise and her with the baby on her arm.[18]

This black man has not completed a response which he is capable of completing. On the other hand, an attempt to help might have resulted in a situation which is not perceived by the woman to be helpful. The following comment from Michele Landsberg could have come from the woman in this example:

"When I'm alone on a New York elevator or subway platform and a black man in a windbreaker enters, I hold my purse tighter. He knows it. I know he knows. The fear, and the reasons for the fear, are poisons to both of us and to all of society."[19]

Circumstances which seem to be the same are often very different depending on the social conditions of those in a circumstance. Examples used in earlier chapters about responding to people who, for one reason or another, are stranded have a decidedly different description depending on who is stranded and who might respond. A woman encountering a man beside a stopped car on a highway is essentially involved in a different circumstance than a man who encounters another man in the same situation.

Social and political factors which make it difficult for people to respond fully to others for fear of being sued, attacked, ridiculed, or rejected are very often out of a person's control. What is paradoxical, however, is that someone may still be morally assessed if he or she does not respond fully. Thomas Nagel writes that "where a significant aspect of what someone does depends on factors beyond his control, yet we continue to treat him in that respect as an object of moral judgment, it can be called moral luck."[20] What is paradoxical about moral luck is that the significance of an individual's response or lack of it is determined by how things turn out. Although the subway example may be an instance of moral luck, circumstances like this do not have to prevail. It is possible for people to have some effect on the reconstruction of social and political life so that circumstances which often paralyse caring responses do not continue to have the same effect.

Social and political factors can affect a caring response in other ways as well. People whose lives are severely restricted by poverty, war, starvation, ignorance, domestic violence, and/or oppression may not have an opportunity to develop important practical and social skills which assist in caring responses. They may also have fewer opportunities to respond to others. Certainly, the bleak circumstances of many peoples' lives make it very difficult for them to be socially active in creating change.

It may be possible for some people to sequester themselves so that they are less affected by circumstance and, by doing so, lead lives which are without blemish. This type of life is morally insignificant, however, if there are few occasions to respond to others. By sequestering oneself, one may avoid situations in which a response may turn out badly but one will also avoid situations in which one's response might turn out well. When there are no caring responses there are also no specific caring desires. If someone has few specific benevolent or just desires, this person is not caring.

I have said that it is not enough for a caring person to desire others' welfare and fair treatment without doing anything to see that others are treated well and fairly. This may involve working toward changing certain oppressive social institutions or it may simply involve equipping oneself with certain skills so that one is able to have an effect on the lives of others when moral situations arise.

Notes

1. By this I am not suggesting that there is such a thing as a singular, essential self. Personal identity is multi-faceted because personal identity depends on relations with others. See John King-Farlow, "Akrasia, Self-Mastery and the Master Self," *Pacific Philosophical Quarterly* 62 (1981): 47-60, for a discussion about how contradictory "personae" might coexist in the same self.
2. William Frankena says in *Ethics*, 2nd. ed. (Englewood Cliffs: Prentice-Hall, 1973), p. 68, that honesty and fidelity are corollaries of benevolence and justice.
3. G. J. Warnock, *The Object of Morality* (London: Methuen 1971), pp. 78-79.
4. David G. Attfield, "Problems with Virtues," *Journal of Moral Education* 7 (1978): 76.
5. R. S. Peters, "Reason and Habit, The Paradox of Moral Education," in *Moral Development and Moral Education* (London: George Allen and Unwin, 1974), p. 57.
6. Stuart Hampshire, *Thought and Action* (London: Chatto and Windus, 1965), pp. 208-222.
7. Lawrence Blum, *Friendship, Altruism and Morality* (London: Routledge and Kegan Paul, 1980), p. 136.
8. Zeno Vendler, "Speaking of Imagination," in *Language, Mind and Brain,* eds. Thomas W. Simon and Robert J. Scholes (Hillsdale, N.J.: Lawrence Erlbaum Associates, 1982), p. 36.
9. Mary Bitner Wiseman, "Empathetic Identification," *American Philosophical Quarterly* 2 (1978): 107.

10. Wiseman, p. 111.
11. For example, John Wilson writes in "The Dishonesty of Moral Educators," in *Ethics in Education* 2 (1985), "morality has to be seen as an independent form of thought with its own set of good reasons . . . [and] not a matter of being a bit less selfish, a bit more cooperative . . ." (p. 3). In "Language and Moral Education," from *The Domain of Moral Education,* eds. D. B. Cochrane, C. M. Hamm, and A. C. Kazipedes (Toronto: OISE Press, 1979), R. M. Hare writes, "I am convinced that if parents first, and then children, understand better the *formal* character of morality, and of the moral concepts, there would be little need to bother, ultimately, about the content of our children's moral principles; for if the form is really and clearly understood, the content will look after itself" (p. 104).
12. L. Daniels et al., *The Elderly* (Toronto: OISE Press, 1978).
13. Alfred Haefner, "The Ethical Syllogism," *Ethics* 71 (1961): 289.
14. Daniel DeNicola, "The Education of the Emotions," in *The Philosophy of Education Society Proceedings* (1979): 215.
15. Bernard Williams, "Morality and the Emotions," in *Problems of the Self* (Cambridge: At the University Press, 1973), p. 225.
16. Warnock, *The Object of Morality,* p. 81.
17. Martin Buber, *Between Man and Man,* trans. Ronald Gregor Smith (London: Kegan Paul, 1947).
18. Jésus Colón, "Little Things are Big," in *Puerto Rican in New York and Other Sketches*. Distributed by Ayer Co., Salem, NH.
19. Michele Landsberg, "Goetz verdict upholds US tradition of extra-legal violence," in *The Globe and Mail* (Saturday, 20 June 1987), p. A2.
20. Thomas Nagel, "Moral Luck," in *Mortal Questions* (Cambridge: Cambridge University Press, 1979), p. 26.

Motivation to Care

In the preceding chapters I have attempted to draw out those components which make up a caring response. Before addressing how someone might become motivated to care, I will briefly summarize these components:

1. *Moral situation.* In order for a caring response to occur there must be a situation in which either someone's welfare or fair treatment is at stake. Not all situations we encounter are like this. To consider every situation to be a moral situation is to trivialize morality.

2. *Appraisal of a moral situation as a moral situation.* We are often so busy or rushed or too self-centred to recognize when someone's welfare or fair treatment is at stake. In order to respond to someone in a moral situation, one must necessarily have an ability to see moral situations as moral situations.

3. *Motivation that those in a moral situation are treated well or fairly.* The focus of one's motivation must be on those in the situation rather than on how a response might enhance oneself, or how one might avoid punishment, or conform to laws, or meet one's religious commitments, and so on.

4. *Practical and/or social skills.* Someone who recognizes a moral situation as a moral situation and desires another's welfare and fair treatment will also often require certain skills in order to act. These skills vary from being able to resuscitate someone to being able to communicate with someone who is troubled.

5. *An action, if an action is possible.* An action is an essential part of a caring response in those situations in which an action is possible.

Sometimes it is impossible to act. Because motivation is also an essential part of a caring response, absence of action in situations in which action is impossible does not preclude a caring response to another.

6. *Emotion*. If a caring person recognizes a moral situation as a moral situation and desires someone's welfare or fair treatment, he or she will experience an emotion during the moral situation and as a result of how the situation is resolved.

If members of a community are to respond with care to each other, attention will need to be paid to each of these components. All members of the community, not just some, must be expected to confront the various moral situations which will arise in the community. They must learn to see moral situations as moral situations and be able to distinguish those moral situations which require fairness from those moral situations which require help. They must acquire skills, including reasoning skills, to be able to adjudicate and help effectively. Most importantly, however, they must come to desire the welfare and fair treatment of others and, by doing so, emotionally respond to them. The purpose of this chapter is to discuss how the components of a caring response can be developed. Of particular importance is how people can be motivated to care.

Some of the components of a caring response and some of the factors which affect these components can be approached systematically by schools. Schools can, for example, assist with the understanding of certain beliefs and with the acquisition of practical and social skills. Other factors, such as imagination, being able to see situations *as* moral situations, and expression of emotion, are less easily developed in a systematic way by schools. Even if all of these factors could be directly affected by schooling, however, we are no closer to achieving caring people. Development of caring people depends on the development of benevolent and just desires.

How does someone come to desire fairly permanently the welfare and fair treatment of others? How does someone become a caring person? Benevolent and just desires are the content of care but benevolent and just desires are not as readily acquired as skills because they do not have a specific subject matter which can be presented and acquired in the same way as skills can be presented and acquired. In the remainder of this chapter I will deal primarily with the relationship of moral education and motivation to care. In doing this I will also say something about the development of beliefs and appraisals. In separate sections I will suggest ways that moral education may affect other factors which are important to a caring response — emotions, reasoning ability, skills, and social factors.

Moral Education and Moral Motivation

> Moral change and moral achievement are slow; we are not . . . able
> suddenly to alter ourselves since we cannot suddenly alter what we
> see and ergo what we desire and are compelled by.[1]

It is not possible simply to decide to be a caring person because it is not possible to desire something merely by deciding to do so. I can decide to try to desire something but actually desiring it does not depend on making a decision. I can try to be a caring person but I will never *be* caring just by deciding to be. What is suggested in the quote from Iris Murdoch is that because "what we desire and are compelled by" is determined by what we regularly give attention to, and attention occurs throughout life, becoming a caring person is a lifelong process.

What someone is, as Murdoch points out, is dependent on a lifelong process of what is looked at and seen by a person. Moral life is not just a series of discrete instances in which an autonomous individual considers a number of alternatives which are unaffected by the rest of his or her life. Any decision someone makes in a moral situation is continuous with the rest of the person's life. What someone does in a particular situation is already determined by what he or she has given attention to most often prior to a moral situation.[2] As Murdoch says, what we give regular attention to builds up structures of value around us so that "by the time the moment of choice has arrived the quality of attention has possibly determined the nature of the act."[3]

We can, of course, attend to objects which will lead us away from caring desires. This "negative looking at" is associated with personal fantasy and is largely responsible for a person's inability to see certain situations unaffected by self-aggrandizement and self-consolation.[4] By seeing a world in which only my fantasies are important, I create what Murdoch calls a "falsifying veil which partially conceals the world"[5] and which, consequently, affects what I desire. For example, I may attend only to my work and console myself when it falters. If I am asked by a student for some attention, my focus on myself and my work allows me to see him as obnoxious. If my attention can be directed away from what Murdoch calls the "fat, relentless ego," I may see the student as insecure. It is only in the latter case that I will help rather than admonish or dismiss.

This process of directing one's attention away from oneself is not an easy process. As I have said, it is not something one can merely decide to do. There is a struggle involved which, as Murdoch says, is to keep one's attention on the real situation and prevent it from "returning surreptitiously to the self with consolations of self-pity, resentment, fantasy and despair."[6] This struggle to direct one's attention away from personal fantasy is a struggle that occurs throughout life and not only during particular moral choices.

Murdoch believes that objects of positive looking at include "anything which alters consciousness in the direction of unselfishness, objectivity and realism."[7] She has a particularly poignant and lovely example of this:

> I am looking out my window in an anxious and resentful state of mind, oblivious of my surroundings, brooding perhaps on some damage to my prestige. Then suddenly I observe a hovering kestral. In a moment everything is altered. The brooding self with its hurt vanity has disappeared. There is nothing now but kestral. And when I return to thinking of the other matter it seems less important. And of course this is something which we may also do deliberately: give attention to nature in order to clear our minds of selfish care.[8]

Murdoch comments that "our ability to act well 'when the time comes' depends partly, perhaps largely, upon the quality of our habitual objects of attention."[9] The very notion of a character trait, as a fairly permanent desire, implies that it be consistent or habitual. In order for someone to become benevolent and just, this person must first make a habit of attending to certain objects and experiences.

What one attends to is of critical importance if caring desires are to expand. It is possible that someone's specific caring desires, although few and weak, can be expanded and intensified until this person has these desires fairly permanently. Even if early habits of attention are toward personal aggrandizement or toward what is destructive or base, it is possible to draw attention away from these objects of "negative looking at." As long as there are individuals about whom one does not care, there is an opportunity to direct attention toward them. And, since it is practically impossible to desire specifically the welfare and fair treatment of all others, this process of directing attention is a process which occurs throughout one's life.

Habitual attention does not preclude being able to understand reasons which justify care. Benevolent and just desires are developed not just by "looking at" certain objects and experiences. They are developed by "seeing" these objects and experiences in a certain way. The process of seeing or appraising requires an ability to assess one's beliefs and having these beliefs requires reflection and understanding. In order to see a situation as one in which another's welfare is affected, for example, someone must have beliefs about what constitutes conflict, beliefs about what constitutes suffering or flourishing, beliefs about others' feelings, and so on. I have described this as part of an important reasoning ability which is the ability to respond to moral motivating reasons.

Beliefs essential to care can be learned in a variety of school subjects. A special moral education class is not required for this. Beliefs about what count as harm, help, conflicts, and fairness can be developed in a myriad of situations which arise in a school day. These include informal situations in which students receive bumps and bruises from playing and doing school projects, from social encounters during school functions, and from classroom encounters with literature or history which provide examples of moral situations. The level of sophistication of discussions about these will, of course, depend on the cognitive ability of students to understand certain important moral concepts.

Drawing attention to situations which exemplify beliefs about care will also help someone see a situation as an instance in which care is appropriate. When a situation arises which might have a number of different interpretations, a teacher can draw attention to features of the situation which make it an instance in which a caring response would be appropriate. Many instances in which others are unhappy or are treated unfairly will be obvious. Often, however, a teacher will need to remember that race, class, gender, or disability may be a factor which is not being noticed. To be blind to the ways in which these can function in social contexts not only eliminates the opportunity to draw students' attention to some very real and important examples of how welfare and fairness can be affected, but it may also serve to perpetuate unfairness or unkindness as the following example shows:

> When teachers feel they are being fair, or even showing favoritism to girls, the empirical evidence shows otherwise. For example, giving 35 percent of one's attention to girls can feel as though one is being unfair to boys. Giving just one third of one's attention to girls can feel as though one is making a significant effort, even compensating girls.[10]

"Gender sensitivity,"[11] as well as sensitivity to race, class, and disability, is essential if a teacher is to direct attention to situations in which care is appropriate and to ensure that there are fewer situations to which students may attend by default which reinforce gender, race, class, or disability bias. A caring teacher must not only desire that others are treated well and fairly; he or she must be actively involved in understanding the subtle ways in which people may be treated poorly and unfairly so that these may be changed. This is so because a caring person is someone who desires that others are actually treated well and fairly. Someone cannot be oblivious to ways in which people can be treated poorly and unfairly and be a caring person.

I have been using a vision metaphor which is based upon Iris Murdoch's notion of attention.[12] I want to extend this metaphor by suggesting that motivation to care consists of a process of having one's eyes opened so that one looks at moral situations and sees them in a certain way.

Having one's eyes opened so that one "looks at" and "sees" may happen through one's own efforts, but it is more likely to happen through the influence of others. People learn about care by seeing the lives and actions of caring people. Someone who is important in one's life can considerably change the significance of what might otherwise go unnoticed. Attempting to see what someone who is admired sees about an enterprise is an important step in the process of attention. Attending to the actions and interests of someone who is significant in one's life, such as a caring teacher, may often be a stronger motivator than any argument used by this teacher.[13] We must, however, be cautious about how charismatic leaders exert their influence. A charismatic leader who is not also caring may, for example, promote hatred toward a group of people. Moreover, even caring people may encourage others to copy their behavior without helping them to understand the importance of this behavior or without helping them to acquire benevolent and just desires.

Caring Emotions

Daniel DeNicola describes four different proposals for education of emotions[14] which I will use to make comments about education of caring emotions.

1. *Education of emotions as suppressing or chanelling emotions.*

The assumption of an educational program designed to suppress emotions is that "an emotional person is immature, maladjusted, and often irrational."[15] I have argued, on the other hand, that emotions are a necessary result of an ability to respond to moral motivating reasons. An educational program designed to assist people to suppress emotions would destroy the informational value of emotions since a sincere display of emotion is a signal to those in a moral situation that someone cares.

R. S. Peters is an advocate of controlling and channelling emotions. "Rather than simply burn with anger, stew in resentment, or wither with grief, the emotionally educated person will produce an aesthetic object, strive for social reform, or otherwise act in a constructive manner. . . ."[16] Although an extreme experience of emotion can be debilitating, emotions do not have to be experienced in this way. Those who tend to have overwhelming experiences of emotion in moral situations must be helped to bring their emotions under control so that a caring response can be completed. In other words, a person who experiences extreme emotion must learn how to control emotion felt so that he or she can either help or adjudicate and so that those in a moral situation are able to discern his or her motivation.

Although caring emotions may sometimes need to be controlled, they do not need to be channelled because caring emotions provide valuable information to those in moral predicaments about an agent's motivation. Immoral emotions (emotions experienced as a result of desires which conflict with desires for welfare and fair treatment of sentient beings) do, on the other hand, need to be controlled and channelled. Human emotions include jealousy, rage, envy, and self-pity, and while it is important to recognize these emotions in oneself and others, moral education is concerned with controlling and channelling them. It is not sufficient merely to redirect and control immoral emotions, however, because as long as someone has these emotions, he or she has immoral desires. Control of immoral emotions must ultimately be concerned with the development of caring desires.

2. *Education of emotions as becoming adept at identifying emotions.*

It is important to be able to recognize when emotions are being experienced by myself or by others. Being able to recognize when I am experiencing an emotion is an important step in coming to understand my own motivation.

Being able to recognize emotions in others is often important in being able to recognize a moral situation. If one is to respond to someone who is grieving, for example, one must be able to recognize grief. Moreover, when one is able to identify emotions felt by others, it is possible to learn the motivation of their responses. Being aware of others' motivation through an understanding of their emotions is important to parents, teachers, friends, and others who might want to help someone become a caring person.

Being able to identify emotions in others is not to learn to have emotions oneself, however. Although important, this approach to education of emotions only involves education of cognitive skills and not actual experience of emotion.

3. *Education of emotions as increasing the justifiability of one's emotions.*

An *experience* of an emotion is justified if one's beliefs and evaluation of these beliefs are justified. A *display* of emotion is justified in terms of appropriate intensity, duration, and sincerity. Someone is not justified in her experience of fear of a flower because beliefs that flowers are harmful are not justified. An emotion can be unjustified in ways corresponding to essential features of an emotion: an unreasonable desire or intensity of desire in light of one's beliefs (baseless or irrational); an unreasonable object of desire (baseless or irrational); unreasonable beliefs about an object (baseless or superstitious); or unreasonable evaluation of an object (abnormal). Education of emotions which focusses on justifiability of emotions must contend with one or more of these conditions.

Display of emotion may also be justified or unjustified. Justifiable display of emotion can be very complex primarily, as I said in the last chapter, because appropriate display of emotion is affected by situational and cultural factors. What is of importance in education of emotional display is that someone is able to express emotion in such a way that those in a moral situation are able to discern one's motivation.

4. *Education of emotions as increasing sensitivity, freshness, scope, and complexity of emotions.*

DeNicola suggests that increasing sensitivity, freshness, scope, and complexity of emotions entails a growth in ability to imagine and express alternative ways of feeling.[17] It is possible to expand the *intensity* of different feelings. It is not clear, however, whether it is possible to increase emotional alternatives. Annette Baier has this to say,

> It is a peculiar but little wondered fact that we can draw up *lists* of feeling possibilities . . . aiming at a completed list, whereas no one would dream of trying to list all the actions, or all the beliefs that are humanly possible. . . . We may discriminate more finely but not discover or invent a wholly new feeling. . . . Whatever we think or do, however exciting the horizons there, and however inventive our expression of our feelings, our feelings themselves remain unoriginal, restricted to the same familiar round.[18]

If the goal of education of emotions is to increase alternative ways of feeling this can, as Baier indicates, only apply to alternative ways to express emotion and not alternative ways of experiencing emotion. Baier wonders why this is so and leaves it as a question. She asks, "Are we necessarily restricted in our feelings . . . , not just contingently restricted, as we are, say, in our auditory powers, and if we are, what explains the necessity? Sociobiological constraints? The very idea of a social animal?"[19] A partial answer to these questions is that one's experience of emotion is necessarily tied to desire and evaluated beliefs so how or what one feels cannot be affected without first affecting what one desires. This does not answer, however, the question why the desires we do have result in a circumscribed range of feelings.

Increasing sensitivity, freshness, scope, and complexity of caring emotions depends upon developing the intensity and scope of benevolent and just desires. Education of caring emotions is primarily concerned, then, with influencing the direction of attention so that benevolent and just desires develop.

Reasoning Abilities

I have said that if someone is caring there are some abilities which this person requires which can be systematically developed in schools. Some reasoning abilities are like this. If, however, someone is not already caring, acquiring moral reasoning abilities will merely be an intellectual ability demonstrable in contrived examples of moral situations. In actual moral situations, if a person is not caring, he or she will not likely use these abilities as part of a caring response.

Since there are three types of moral reasoning abilities — abilities associated with moral motivating reasons, adjudicating reasons, and justifying reasons — education of reasoning abilities must be concerned with each.

As I have already discussed, the development of an ability to respond to moral motivating reasons depends on the development of caring desires, beliefs, and appraisals. An ability to provide adjudicating reasons is an ability to provide relevant reasons when making decisions in a situation which requires adjudication. An ability to recognize justifying reasons is an ability to acknowledge that a particular situation is a moral situation.

Providing relevant reasons and recognizing reasons which justify certain situations as instances of particular enterprises are general reasoning abilities: they are not specific to moral situations. These general reasoning abilities can be developed in critical thinking or informal logic courses. Including both non-moral and moral examples in these types of courses is preferable to structuring separate courses designed to develop moral reasoning ability. This is because the separation of moral reasoning ability into moral education classes suggests that moral education can be reduced to an ability to reason through certain moral problems. This is false.

An alternative would be to have applied ethics classes in which students are introduced to both moral reasoning abilities and contemporary ethical issues. There is an important difference between classes in applied ethics and classes in moral education. The former may present moral and social theory to students with the purpose of having students recognize how they might be applied to actual ethical issues. Moral education, on the other hand, must necessarily be concerned that students become morally educated. I have indicated that I believe this to be an impossible task in a classroom setting. Ethics courses, on the other hand, may provide an opportunity for students to take note of and attend to what is relevant to a moral life.

Skills and Know-how

Scheduled sessions in schools can assist the acquisition of both practical and social skills. These scheduled classes should not be moral education classes since it is too easily inferred that acquisition of these skills is all there is to moral education. It is preferable to introduce these skills either as distinct courses or as parts of other courses. Life saving skills, for example, are an important part of health or physical education courses. Artificial respiration is better included as part of a swimming class than as part of a class in moral education.

Social skills are better enhanced in the social atmosphere of the school than in contrived encounters in a classroom. Interpersonal encounters will occur authentically during co-operative and competitive games, school choirs, drama clubs, and other school activities. Teachers can facilitate acquisition of social skills in these situations by drawing attention to instances in which better communication might help alleviate differences or, for example, by helping students involve those who might be on the periphery of a group. Teachers can sensitize students to how lives are often very different as a result of race, class, gender, or disability, and that one or more of these factors may be operating when others are excluded from some social encounters. To be sensitive to these is to become skilled in asking whether they are affecting a situation in any important way and in asking whether one's assessment of a situation contributes to gender, race, class, or disability bias.[20]

Social Factors

Proximity and circumstance are social factors which affect the development of caring people. Each can, in turn, be affected only indirectly by education. Education cannot change the physical proximity of people, although it can, at least, contribute to making others more morally proximate. By this I mean that education can help to improve awareness of others who are physically distant. Being aware of others is essential if one is to care about them.

Education can be of assistance in the direction of attention toward certain exemplary objects and events. Education is a very slow process, however, when it comes to changing the abysmal circumstances of some people's lives in which attention is consistently on poverty and exploitation. It is not a very helpful solution to those living in poverty that they shift their attention to exemplary lives and events. In many cases only a massive redistribution of resources would make it possible for these people to have an opportunity for "positive looking at." Murdoch's person of attention struggles to direct attention away from self-indulgence. People without food, shelter, and safety must focus their attention on satisfying their need for these, which is anything but self-indulgent. And, as long as females and males are expected to have different desires, including different moral desires, and social institutions operate to ensure that this will occur, it is unlikely that fully caring people will develop. If social structures continue to prepare women and men for different moral tasks, our society will be composed of nurturing, self-sacrificing, and dependent women and separating, autonomous men. In other words, full functioning caring people who desire others' welfare and fair treatment in a community of other caring people will be rare.

Because moral education takes place beyond the school walls as well as within them and, because what many attend to beyond the school walls is dismal, if people are to be motivated to care, there must be changes made to social and political conditions which make care difficult. Care is not, as Noddings would have it, circumscribed by instances involving friends and family. One can also directly care for others outside these circles. One can care, as well, about welfare and fair treatment in situations in which people other than oneself act. If someone cares that others are treated well and fairly in all situations in which others' welfare or fair treatment is affected, this person is committed to altering those social institutions and interactions that work against achieving welfare and fair treatment. Noddings is correct that one caring person could not possibly ensure that everyone is treated well or fairly. But a caring person can work toward changing formal and informal institutions which affect whether others respond well and fairly.

Caring that others are treated well and fairly in those situations in which one cannot act also entails a commitment to moral education. Since a caring person cannot directly desire everyone's welfare and fair treatment but believes that everyone should be treated well and fairly, it is essential that others are caring. Commitment to moral education is a commitment to establishing moral environments to which people can attend. As I have said, schools can be one of these environments but they are only one of many environments. The motivation of people to care will not occur in isolated moral education courses in schools. Even if a moral education class is able to direct attention, it will be ineffectual if the rest of a school environment is devoid of objects of moral attention. Furthermore, achieving a school environment in which positive objects of attention are plentiful will only have a small effect if the students' home and social life is otherwise. Schools are a small, albeit important, part of developing motivation to care. But a school cannot possibly fully develop an individual's character, because a school environment does not include all of our attentional experiences either in a given day or in a lifetime.

Summary Comment

Care as moral motivation and motivation to care are both complex notions. Understanding each is valuable because care is essential to moral life. Clarity about care as moral motivation and clarity about motivation to care guards against reductionism in understanding care and its motivation. Philosophical analysis is essential to this understanding but, once understood, analysis of care is not to be confused with being a caring person. One need not be able to analyse care in order to care.

Notes

1. Iris Murdoch, *The Sovereignty of Good* (London: Routledge and Kegan Paul, 1970), p. 39.
2. Murdoch, p. 17.
3. Murdoch, p. 67.
4. Murdoch, p. 59.
5. Murdoch, p. 84.
6. Murdoch, p. 91.
7. Murdoch, p. 84.
8. Murdoch, p. 84.
9. Murdoch, p. 56.
10. Barbara Houston, "Gender Freedom and the Subtleties of Sexist Education," *Educational Theory* 35 (1985): In this passage Houston relies on Dale Spender's *Invisible Women: The Schooling Scandal* (London: Writers and Readers Publishing Cooperative Society, 1982).
11. Jane Roland Martin, "The Ideal of the Educated Person," *Educational Theory* 31 (1981): 97-109.
12. While this vision metaphor is particularly important to understanding how people come to desire others' welfare and fair treatment, other sensory metaphors are also useful to understanding moral life. A hearing metaphor, with its emphasis on voice, for example, has been used effectively to describe women's experience of moral life. Carol Gilligan uses a hearing-voice metaphor in *In A Different Voice* and Belenky et al. use this metaphor in *Women's Ways of Knowing: The Development of Self, Voice, and Mind* (New York: Basic Books, Inc., 1986). I disagree, however, with the view of Belenky et al. that distance between people is implied when using a vision metaphor to describe relations. They write,
    "Visual metaphors encourage standing at a distance to get a proper view, removing . . . subject and object from a sphere of possible intercourse. Unlike the eye, the ear operates by registering subtle change. Unlike the eye, the ear requires closeness between subject and object. Unlike seeing, speaking and listening suggest dialogue and interaction." (p. 18)
    The ear can connect people in the way described here but hearing does not always connect people. Nor does seeing always create distance, as Murdoch's example of being engrossed when attending to the kestral illustrates so well.

13. Kenneth Pahel, "Moral Motivation," in *The Domain of Education,* edited by D. B. Cochrane, C. M. Hamm, and A. C. Kazipedes (Toronto: OISE Press, 1979), p. 137.
14. Daniel DeNicola, "The Education of the Emotions," in *Philosophy of Education Proceedings* (1979): 210-223.
15. DeNicola, p. 213.
16. DeNicola, p. 214.
17. DeNicola, p. 216.
18. Annette Baier, *Postures of the Mind: Essays on Mind and Morals* (Minneapolis: University of Minnesota Press, 1985), pp. 123-24.
19. Baier, p. 124.
20. Just how difficult the acquisition of this skill is has become apparent to me in my own writing.

# Bibliography

Alston, William. "Toward a Logical Geography of Personality Traits and Deeper Lying Personality Characteristics." In *Mind, Science and History,* edited by H. E. Keifer and M. K. Munitz, pp. 59-92. Albany, N.Y.: State University of New York Press, 1970.

Arnold, Magda. *The Nature of Emotion.* New York: Penguin Books, 1968.

Attfield, David G. "Problems with Virtues." *Journal of Moral Education* 7 (1978): 75-80.

Baier, Annette. *Postures of the Mind: Essays on Mind and Morals.* Minneapolis: University of Minnesota Press, 1985.

Baier, Annette. "Hume, the Women's Moral Theorist." In *Women and Moral Theory,* edited by Eva Feder Kittay and Diana T. Meyers, pp. 37-55. Totowa, N.J.: Rowman and Littlefield, 1987.

Baier, Kurt. *The Moral Point of View.* New York: Random House, 1965.

Baron, Marcia. "The Alleged Moral Repugnance of Acting from Duty." *The Journal of Philosophy* 81 (1984): 197-220.

Beehler, Rodger. "Reasons for Being Moral." *Analysis* 33 (1972): 12-21.

Beehler, Rodger. *Moral Life.* Oxford: Basil Blackwell, 1978.

Belenky, M. F.; Clinchy, B. M.; Goldberger, N. R.; Tarule, J. M. *Women's Ways of Knowing: The Development of Self, Voice, and Mind.* New York: Basic Books, Inc., 1986.

Benhabib, Selya. "The Generalized and the Concrete Other." In *Women and Moral Theory,* edited by Eva Feder Kittay and Diana T. Meyers, pp. 154-77. Totowa, N.J.: Rowman and Littlefield, 1987.

Bentham, Jeremy. *Introduction to the Principles of Morals and Legislation.* Introduction by Laurence J. Lafleur. New York: Hafner Publishing Co., 1948.

Blum, Lawrence. "Compassion." In *Explaining Emotions,* edited by Amelie Rorty, pp. 507-17. Berkeley: University of California Press, 1980.

Blum, Lawrence. *Friendship, Altruism and Morality.* London: Routledge and Kegan Paul, 1980.

Blum, Lawrence. "Kant's and Hegel's Moral Rationalism: A Feminist Perspective." *Canadian Journal of Philosophy* 12 (1982): 287-300.

Boyd, Dwight. "Careful Justice or Just Caring: A Response to Gilligan." In *Philosophy of Education Society Proceedings* (1982): 63-69.

Brandt, Richard. "The Psychology of Benevolence and Its Implications for Philosophy." *Journal of Philosophy* 73 (1976): 429-53.

Brandt, Richard. "Traits of Character: A Conceptual Analysis." *American Philosophical Quarterly* (1970): 23-37.

Buber, Martin. *Between Man and Man.* Translated by Donald Gregor Smith. London: Kegan Paul, 1947.

Cancian, Francesca. "The Feminization of Love." *Signs: Journal of Women in Culture and Society* 11 (1986): 692-709.

Chodorow, Nancy. *The Reproduction of Mothering: Psychoanalysis and the Sociology of Gender.* Berkeley: University of California Press, 1978.

Colón, Jésus. "Little Things are Big." In *Puerto Rican in New York and Other Sketches.* Distributed by Ayer Co., Salem, NH.

Daniels, L.; Douglas, L.; Oliver, C.; and Wright, I., eds. *The Elderly.* Toronto: OISE Press, 1978.

Dearden, R. F.; Hirst, P. H.; and Peters, R. S., eds. *Education and the Development of Reason.* London: Routledge and Kegan Paul, 1972.

DeFaveri, Ivan. "Moral Education: The Risk of Over-Simplification." *The Alberta Journal of Educational Research* 25 (1979): 294-306.

DeNicola, Daniel. "The Education of the Emotions." In *The Philosophy of Education Society Proceedings,* 1979, pp. 210-223.

Dunlop, Francis. "The Education of the Emotions." *Journal of the Philosophy of Education* 18 (1984): 245-55.

Falk, W. D. "Action Guiding Reasons." *Journal of Philosophy* 60 (1963): 702-718.

Feinberg, Joel. *Right, Justice and the Bounds of Liberty: Essays in Social Philosophy.* Princeton: Princeton University Press, 1980.

Flanagan, Owen. "Virtue, Sex, and Gender: Some Philosophical Reflections of the Moral Psychology Debate." *Ethics* 92 (1982): 499-512.

Flanagan, Owen, and Jackson, Kathryn. "Justice, Care and Gender: The Kohlberg-Gilligan Debate Revised." *Ethics* 97 (1987): 622-37.

Fingarette, Herbert. *Self-Deception.* London: Routledge and Kegan Paul, 1969.

Ford, Maureen. "Gender-Sensitive Education: Reconsidering Jane Roland Martin's Critique of the 'Educated Man' Ideal." M. A. thesis, University of Toronto, 1987.

Ford, Maureen. "Gender-Bending is Political: Gender Sensitive Education Reconsidered." A paper presented to the Canadian Society of Women in Philosophy and the Canadian Women's Studies Association Learned Society Meeting, Hamilton, Ontario, 25 May 1987.

Frankena, William. *Ethics*. 2nd. ed. Englewood Cliffs: Prentice-Hall, Inc., 1973.

Gilligan, Carol. *In A Different Voice: Psychological Theory and Women's Development*. Cambridge, Mass.: Harvard University Press, 1982.

Gilligan, Carol. "New Maps of Development: New Visions of Education." In *Philosophy of Education Society Proceedings*, 1982, pp. 47-62.

Gilligan, Carol. "Moral Orientation and Moral Development." In *Women and Moral Theory*, edited by Eva Feder Kittay and Diana T. Meyers, pp. 19-33. Totowa, N.J.: Rowman and Littlefield, 1987.

Gould, Stephen. *Ever Since Darwin*. New York: Norton, 1977.

Gouldner, Alvin. "The Norm of Reciprocity: A Preliminary Statement." *American Sociological Review* 25 (1960): 161-78.

Grimshaw, Jean. *Philosophy and Feminist Thinking*. Minneapolis: University of Minnesota Press, 1986.

Haefner, Alfred. 'The Ethical Syllogism." *Ethics* 71 (1961): 289-95.

Hampshire, Stuart. *Thought and Action*. London: Chatto and Windus, 1965.

Harding, Sandra. "Is Gender a Variable in Conceptions of Rationality? A Survey of Issues." *Dialectica* 36 (1982): 225-42.

Hare, R. M. "Language and Moral Education." In *The Domain of Moral Education*, edited by D. B. Cochrane, C. M. Hamm, and A. C. Kazipedes, pp. 89-106. Toronto: OISE Press, 1979.

Heyd, David. *Supererogation: Its Status In Ethical Theory*. Cambridge: Cambridge University Press, 1982.

Hearn, Jeff, and Wendy Parkin, P. "Gender and Organization: A Selective Review and Critique of a Neglected Area." *Organization Studies* 4 (1983): 219-42.

Hoffman, Martin. "Empathy, Role-Taking, Guilt, and Development of Altruistic Motives." In *Moral Development and Behavior*, edited by Thomas Lickman, pp. 124-43. New York: Holt, Rinehart and Winston, 1976.

Houston, Barbara. "Gender Freedom and the Subtleties of Sexist Education." *Educational Theory* 35 (1985): 359-69.

Hume, David. *A Treatise of Human Nature*, edited by L. A. Selby-Bigge, 2nd ed., Oxford: Clarendon Press, 1888.

Jagger, Alison. "Human Biology in Feminist Theory: Sexual Equality Reconsidered." In *Beyond Domination: New Perspectives in Women and Philosophy*, edited by Carol C. Gould, pp. 21-42. Totowa, N.J.: Rowman and Allanheld, 1984.

James, William. *Principles of Psychology*. Vol. II. New York: Macmillan, 1890.

Kant, Immanuel. *Lectures on Ethics.* Translated by L. Infield. New York: Harper and Row, 1963.

Kanter, Rosabeth Moss. *Men and Women of the Corporation.* New York: Basic Books, 1977.

King-Farlow, John. "Akrasia, Self-Mastery and the Master Self." *Pacific Philosophical Quarterly* 62 (1981): 47-60.

Kohlberg, Lawrence. "From Is to Ought." In *Cognitive Development and Epistemology,* edited by Theodore Mischel, pp. 151-235. New York: Academic Press, 1971.

Kohlberg, Lawrence. "Education for Justice: A Modern Statement of the Platonic View." In *Moral Education: Five Lectures,* edited by N. F. Sizer and T. R. Sizer, pp. 57-83. Cambridge, Mass.: Harvard University Press, 1970.

Landsberg, Michele. "Goetz verdict upholds U.S. tradition of extra-legal violence." In *The Globe and Mail,* Saturday, 20 June 1987, A2.

Lloyd, Genevieve. *The Man of Reason: Male and Female in Western Philosophy.* London: Methuen, 1984.

Locke, Don. "Beliefs, Desires and Reasons for Action." *American Philosophical Quarterly* 19 (1982): 241-49.

Lyons, William. *Emotion.* Cambridge: Cambridge University Press, 1980.

Malikail, J. S. "A Philosophy of Mind Adequate for Discourse on Morality: Iris Murdoch's Critique." *Journal of Educational Thought* 15 (1981): 61-72.

Marcel, Gabriel. *The Philosophy of Martin Buber,* edited by Paul Schlipp and Maurice Friedman. Lasalle, Illinois: Open Court Publishing Co., 1967.

Martin, Jane Roland. "Needed: A New Paradigm for Liberal Education." In *The Eightieth N.S.S.E. Yearbook.* Chicago: University of Chicago Press, 1981.

Martin, Jane Roland. "The Ideal of the Educated Person." *Educational Theory* 31 (1981): 97-109.

Martin, Jane Roland. *Reclaiming a Conversation: The Ideal of the Educated Woman.* New Haven: Yale University Press, 1985.

Mayeroff, Milton. *On Caring.* New York: Perennial Library, 1971.

Mercer, Philip. *Sympathy and Ethics.* Oxford: At the Clarendon Press, 1971.

Meyers, Diane T., and Kittay, Eva Feder, eds. *Women and Moral Theory.* Totowa, N.J.: Rowman and Littlefield, 1987.

Midgley, Mary. *Animals and Why They Matter.* New York: Penguin Books, 1983.

Morgan, Kathryn Pauly. "Women and Moral Madness." A paper presented to the Canadian Society of Women in Philosophy, Montreal, 1984.

Morgan, Kathryn Pauly. "Romantic Love, Altruism, and Self-Respect." In *Women and Men: Interdisciplinary Readings in Gender,* edited by Greta Hoffmann Nemiroff, pp. 264-89. Toronto: Fitzhenry and Whiteside, 1987.

Murdoch, Iris. *The Sovereignty of Good.* London: Routledge and Kegan Paul, 1970.

Nagel, Thomas. *The Possibility of Altruism*. Oxford: Clarendon Press, 1970.

Nagel, Thomas. "Moral Luck." In *Mortal Questions*, pp. 24-38. Cambridge: Cambridge University Press, 1979.

Nagel, Thomas. "Subjective and Objective." In *Mortal Questions*, pp. 196-213. Cambridge: Cambridge University Press, 1979.

Nagel, Thomas. "What Is It Like to Be a Bat?" In *Mortal Questions*, pp. 165-80. Cambridge: Cambridge University Press, 1979.

Nicholson, Linda. "Women, Morality and History." *Social Research* 50 (1983): 514-36.

Noddings, Nel. "Caring." *Journal of Curriculum Theorizing* (1981): 139-48.

Noddings, Nel. *Caring: A Feminine Approach to Ethics and Moral Education*. Berkeley: University of California Press, 1984.

Nowell-Smith, P. H. *Ethics*. Harmondsworth: Penguin Books, 1954.

Ortega y Gasset, José. *The Dehumanization of Art*. New York: Doubleday and Co., Anchor Books, 1956.

Pahel, Kenneth. "Moral Motivation." In *The Domain of Moral Education*, edited by D. B. Cochrane, C. M. Hamm, and A. C. Kazipedes, pp. 135-44. Toronto: OISE Press, 1979.

Peters, R. S. "Motivation, Emotion and the Conceptual Schemes of Common Sense." In *Psychology and Ethical Development: A Collection of Articles on Psychological Theories, Ethical Development and Human Understanding*, pp. 87-118. London: George Allen and Unwin, Ltd., 1974.

Peters, R. S. "Reason and Habit: The Paradox of Moral Education." In *Moral Development and Moral Education*, pp. 45-60. London: George Allen and Unwin, 1974.

Pitcher, G. "Emotion." In *Education and the Development of Reason*, edited by R. F. Dearden, C. H. Hirst, and R. S. Peters, pp. 368-87. London: Routledge and Kegan Paul, 1972.

Rawls, John. *A Theory of Justice*. Cambridge: The Belknap Press of Harvard University, 1971.

Ross, W. D. *The Right and the Good*. Oxford: Clarendon Press, 1930.

Rosthal, Robert. "Moral Weakness and Remorse." *Mind* 76 (1967): 576-79.

Shaffer, Jerome. "An Assessment of Emotion." *American Philosophical Quarterly* 20 (1983): 161-73.

Scheman, Naomi. "On Sympathy." *The Monist* 62 (1979): 320-329.

Shogan, Debra. "Review of Nel Noddings's *Caring: A Feminine Approach to Ethics and Moral Education*." *Canadian Journal of Feminist Ethics* 2 (1986): 21-24.

Shogan, Debra. "Moral Education in Schools: Theory into Practice." *New Education* 8 (1986): 36-45.

Shogan, Debra. "Moral Agency, Gender and the Relationship of Rationality to

Emotions." A paper presented to the Canadian Society of Women in Philosophy and the Canadian Women's Studies Association Learned Society, Hamilton, Ontario, 25 May 1987.

Shogan, Debra. "Education of Moral Emotions." A paper presented to the Canadian Association of Foundations Education Learned Society, Hamilton, Ontario, 3 June 1987.

Spender, Dale. *Invisible Women: The Schooling Scandal.* London: Writers and Readers Publishing Cooperative Society, 1982.

Stocker, Michael. "The Schizophrenia of Modern Ethical Theories." *The Journal of Philosophy* 63 (1976): 453-66.

Teuber, Andrea. "Simone Weil: Equality as Compassion." *Philosophy and Phenomenological Research* 43 (1982): 221-37.

Toulmin, Stephen. *An Examination of the Place of Reason in Ethics.* Cambridge: University Press, 1964.

Urmson, J. O. "Saints and Heroes." In *Essays in Moral Philosophy,* edited by A. I. Melden, pp. 198-216. Seattle: University of Washington Press, 1958.

Vendler, Zeno. "Speaking of Imagination." In *Language, Mind and Brain,* edited by Thomas W. Simon and Robert J. Scholes, pp. 35-43. Hillsdale, N.J.: Lawrence Erlbaum Associates, 1982.

Warnock, G. J. *The Object of Morality.* London: Methuen and Co. Ltd., 1971.

Whitbeck, Carolyn. "A Different Reality: Feminist Ontology." In *Beyond Domination: New Perspectives on Women and Philosophy,* edited by Carol C. Gould, pp. 64-88. Totowa, N.J.: Rowman and Allanheld, 1984.

Williams, Bernard. *Morality: An Introduction to Ethics.* New York: Harper Torchbooks, 1972.

Williams, Bernard. "Ethical Consistency." In *Problems of the Self,* pp. 166-86. Cambridge: Cambridge University Press, 1973.

Williams, Bernard. "Morality and the Emotions." In *Problems of the Self,* pp. 207-229. Cambridge: Cambridge University Press, 1973.

Williams, Bernard. "Persons, Character and Morality." In *The Identities of Persons,* edited by Amelie Rorty, pp. 197-216. Berkeley: University of California Press, 1976.

Williams, Bernard. "Moral Luck." In *Moral Luck: Philosophical Papers 1973-1980,* pp. 20-39. Cambridge: Cambridge University Press, 1981.

Wilson, John. "The Dishonesty of Moral Educators." *Ethics in Education* 2 (1985): 3.

Wiseman, Mary Bitner. "Empathetic Identification." *American Philosophical Quarterly* 2 (1978): 107-113.

Wolf, Susan. "Moral Saints." *The Journal of Philosophy* 77 (1982): 419-39.

 **Index**